ER, IN INDIA OCCIDENTALI·

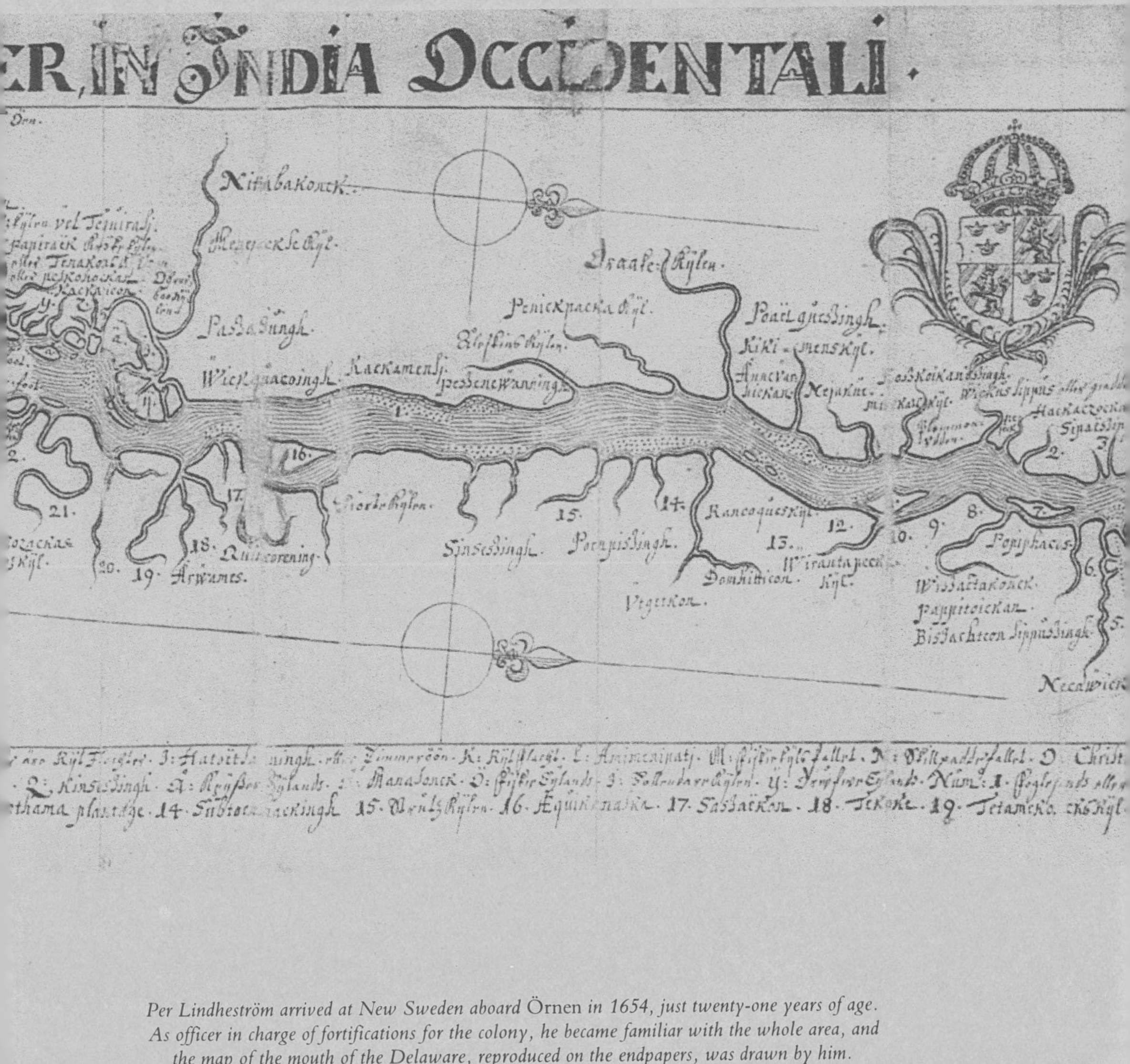

Per Lindheström arrived at New Sweden aboard Örnen in 1654, just twenty-one years of age.
As officer in charge of fortifications for the colony, he became familiar with the whole area, and
the map of the mouth of the Delaware, reproduced on the endpapers, was drawn by him.
Swedish forts and buildings are marked on both sides.

SWEDES IN NORTH AMERICA
1638 – 1988

STREIFFERT & CO BOKFÖRLAG HB
BOX 5098, S-102 42 STOCKHOLM, SWEDEN

Copyright © 1988 Sten Carlsson
Jacket illustration: Claes Forsslöf
Design: Christina von Sivers
Copy editor: Turlough Johnston
Manufactured in Sweden by Ljungföretagen, Örebro 1988
ISBN 91-7886-028-8

Swedes in North America

1638 — 1988

Technical, Cultural, and Political Achievements

Sten Carlsson

Streiffert

CONTENTS

INTRODUCTION

Of all the European immigrant groups that have contributed to the tremendous development of the North American continent since the sixteenth century, the Swedes are one of the oldest — outdistanced only by the British, the Spaniards, the French, and the Dutch. The earliest Swedish settlement was established in 1638 on the Delaware, although it is possible that some Swedes may have settled in, say, New Amsterdam (New York) before that.

In March, 1638, only eighteen years after the Pilgrim Fathers landed in Massachusetts on the *Mayflower,* two Swedish ships sailed up the Delaware to make a landfall at what is now Wilmington, Delaware. They were *Kalmar Nyckel* ("Key of Kalmar" — Kalmar being a town on the east coast of Sweden) and *Fågel Grip* ("Bird Griffin"). Shortly afterwards, a company protected by Christina, Queen of Sweden, purchased a large territory from five Indian chiefs and named it *Nya Sverige* ("New Sweden").

By 1655, the colony was lost to the Dutch. The number of Swedes remained quite small, but despite this the Swedish settlements, which lay in the present states of Delaware, Pennsylvania, and New Jersey, retained their ethnic character. Rather little migration took place from the area, but one such movement was made to Maryland.

Contacts with the mother country, especially on the ecclesiastical level, were maintained until the end of the eighteenth century. By that time, assimilation into the American way of life had advanced quite far, and it can be deemed complete by the first decades of the nineteenth century.

Scarcely had the Swedishness of the early settlements on the Delaware disappeared when new Swedish settlements took root, mainly in the Midwest. These had significantly greater dimensions than had those on the Delaware. Between 1845 and 1930, about 1 1/4 million Swedes emigrated to North America. More than 1 million remained there the rest of their lives, and their descendants have been numerous. In the 1980 census, 4.3 million Americans declared that their ancestry was totally or partially Swedish. Apart from that, there were some hundred thousand Americans of Swedish descent who simply said that their background was Scandinavian. If we add a hundred thousand Canadians who have Swedish origins to this figure, and adjust it upwards for the many Americans who did not declare or were not aware of their Swedish origins, we can say that there are over 5 million North Americans with Swedish ancestry living in North America today. This at a time when there are only 8 1/2 million inhabitants, 1 million of them with no Swedish ancestry at all, living in Sweden. In other words, around 40 percent of the descendants of the people who lived in Sweden around 1850 now have their homes in North America.

This means that a sizeable part of modern Swedish achievement has taken place on the other side of the Atlantic from Sweden. Should we turn the question round and ask what contributions Swedes have made to the history and development of the North American continent, the proportions would be quite different, since Swedes and their descendants have never accounted for more than two percent of the population of North America. Nevertheless, this small group has left a definite mark on the history of the continent. This book will describe the activities of the Swedes in North America, highlighting the areas in which they have contributed most to the progress of the continent. Consequently, special attention must be paid to those Swedish Americans who have been successful in the new country and have thus influenced its progress in such fields as technology, communication, culture, and politics.

Beyond those mentioned by name, we consider the fate and influence of a great number of men and women who have formed the second rank of Swedish Americans, among them whole groups of different categories that must be regarded as typical of the Swedish American population. All of them have contributed to the formation of a complete picture of Swedish American achievement. Those who failed to make it in their new homeland and those who, for some reason or other, simply disappeared from the annals of history, are not forgotten, even though knowledge of them is, for obvious reasons, limited. This book is not an heroic epos but a concrete account of important historical realities.

THE EARLY COLONIZATION

THE SWEDISH AND FINNISH COLONISTS ON THE DELAWARE

During the first decades of the seventeenth century, the kingdom of Sweden, small though it was, developed into a great power. Under the leadership of Gustavus Adolphus (died in 1632) and his chancellor, Axel Oxenstierna (died in 1654), the Swedes built up an efficient administration and managed to exploit the internal strife in the neighboring states. Through the Treaty of Stolbova in 1617, Sweden forced Russia to hand over sovereignty of the inner parts of the Gulf of Finland, which include the territory around present-day Leningrad. The northern shore of the Gulf, which comprises southern Finland, had belonged to Sweden since the twelfth and thirteenth centuries, and the southern shore, which comprises Estonia with its capital Reval (Tallinn), had voluntarily annexed itself to the Swedish crown. In 1629, northern Latvia, with its commercial center Riga, was incorporated into the Swedish monarchy at the Armistice of Altmark, between Sweden and Poland. Furthermore, Sweden was to control for a period of six years some Prussian ports, which provided the country with considerable income, corresponding to about thirty percent of the nation's normal income. When, however, the Armistice expired in 1635, Sweden's position had been weakened through the death of Gustavus Adolphus as well as through setbacks in the Thirty Years' War, and Sweden had to give up the ports. This meant, as

Oxenstierna so drastically pointed out, that the country had lost half of its power.

Oxenstierna and his ministers now had to look for other sources of income, and the virgin territories on the banks of the Delaware in the New World seemed full of promise, even if their hopes of the possibilities offered by the beaver-skin and tobacco trades in North America were undoubtedly exaggerated.

The establishment of a Swedish colony in this territory was originally carried out with the cooperation of Dutch merchants, but very soon the colony was a purely Swedish enterprise. At that time, Atlantic passages were fraught with hardship and many died en route, so the Swedish government had difficulty in recruiting colonists. Some soldiers were commandeered into taking part, while convicts who volunteered to go had their sentences commuted to a certain number of years in the colony. Adultery, stealing, and the destruction of forests were typical crimes for which this possibility was offered. Finns who had settled in the forests of Värmland and neighboring provinces and who had aroused the displeasure of the authorities were often sent, too, being more or less recommended to emigrate voluntarily to "the precious and fertile" colony, which was said to be covered by beautiful and valuable forests inhabited by many animals that provided an extra source of food.

As time went by, however, it became easier to recruit emigrants, and North America became more and more attractive. In 1649 and 1652, groups of Finns applied to be sent to New Sweden, and in 1654, when a major expedition set sail from Göteborg, over a hundred families were left behind, as there was no room on board for them.

Between 1637 and 1655, twelve expeditions left the home country for the colony, and all but two reached the destination safely. One of the two was shipwrecked in the West Indies in 1649, while the other was confiscated in New Amsterdam in

NORWAY
FINLAND
KEXHOLMS LÄN
Vasa
Kexsholm
SWEDEN
Gävle
Öregrund
Åbo
Helsinki
Ladoga
Nyen
Stolbova
Uppsala
Åland
Teusina
INGRIA
Stockholm
Vaxholm
Reval
Narva
Jama
Ivangorod
Novgorod
ESTONIA
Norrköping
Dagö
Hapsal
Dorpat
RUSSIA
Pernau
Gotland
Ösel
Pskov
LIVONIA
Windau
Riga
Kirkholm
Kalmar
DENMARK
Öland
KURLAND
Libau
BALTIC SEA
Memel
LITHUANIA
Bornholm
Putzig
Königsberg
Danzig
PRUSSIA
0   100   200   300   400
KILOMETRES

1654. But the total number of emigrants was rather small — about 800 in all arrived at the colony.

The majority of emigrants came from Stockholm, Uppland, Västergötland (which included Gothenburg), the Finnish areas of central Sweden, and from Finland itself. A small group came from Germany and the Netherlands. Strangely enough, one of the emigrants that sailed in 1638 was a negro slave from Angola called Antonius. He is later mentioned, in 1654, and then under the name of Swartz (*the black*). By that time, he was probably emancipated.

The social background of the colonists was varied. Rather many were noblemen, clergymen, or other persons of standing. When compared with the total population at home, these categories were over-represented in New Sweden at the time. However, the great majority of the emigrants came from a broader stratum of society — they were craftsmen, soldiers, small farmers, farmhands, etc. In the beginning, New Sweden was a military colony, but it soon became an agrarian settlement with an increasing number of "freemen", that is, farmers.

The convicts were at all times in the minority. According to one source in 1702, they were discriminated against by the other colonists. This may have been true to a degree, but many ex-convicts were to reach positions of respect in the colony. Per Larsson Cock, said to have been born or grown up in Bångsta in

---

The Swedish monarchy, 1635. Northern Estonia was incorporated in the monarchy in 1561, and Narva was conquered in 1581. Kexholms län ("county") and Ingria were gained at the Peace of Stolbova in 1617, Livonia at the Armistice of Altmark in 1629. The control of some Prussian harbors, gains in 1629, was lost in 1635. Later on, in 1645 and 1658, seven provinces (Skåne, Blekinge, Halland, Bohuslän, Gotland, Jämtland, and Härjedalen) were taken from Denmark-Norway.

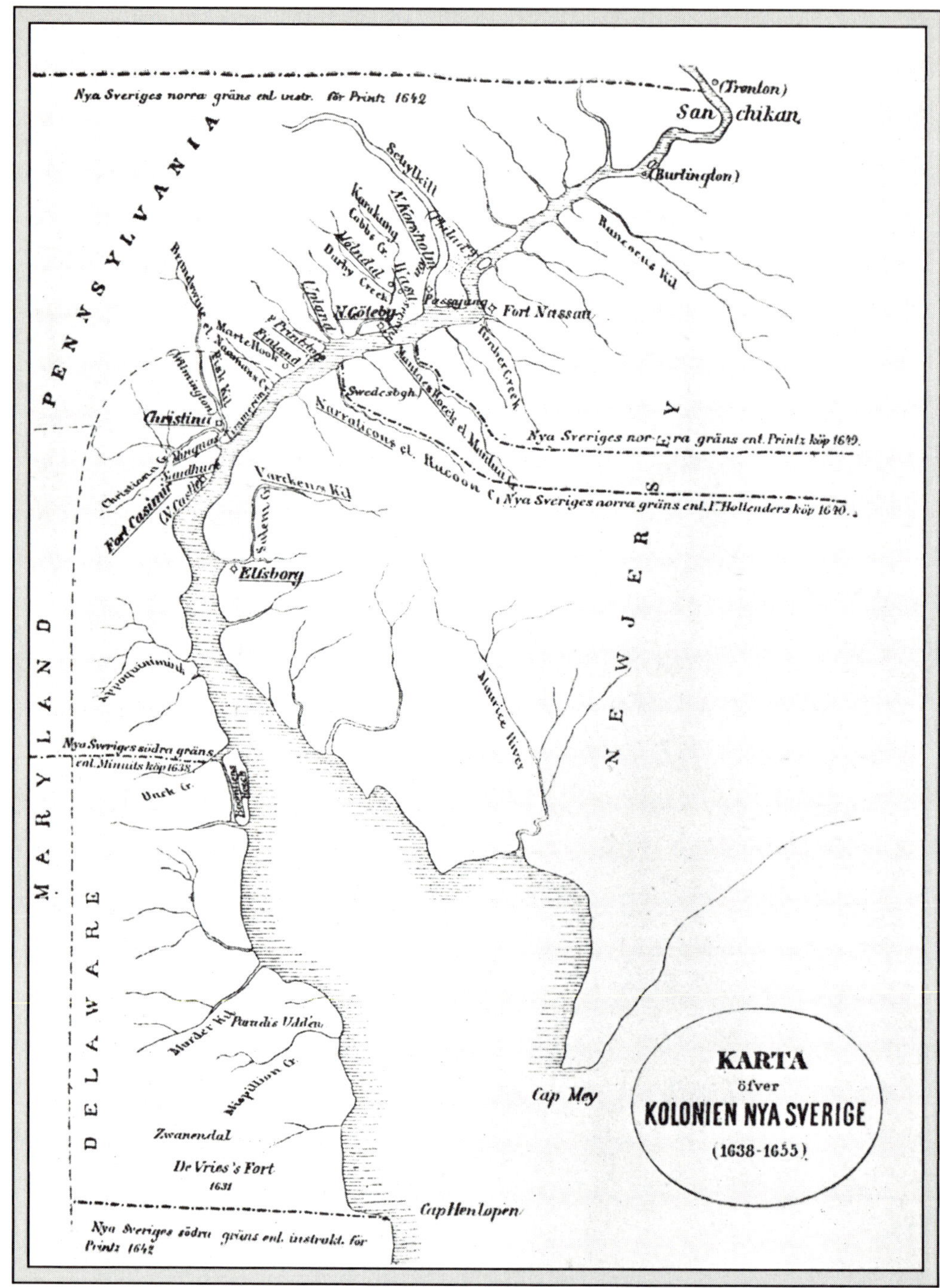
Nya Sveriges norra gräns enl. instr. för Printz 1642
(Trenton)
San chikan
(Burlington)
PENSYLVANIA
Schuylkill
Karakung
N. Korsholm
Cobbs Cr.
Molndal
Finland
Durby Creek
Upland
N. Göteby
Passajung
Fort Nassau
Raccoon Kil
Brandewine el. Fiskekil
Marte Hook
Printstorp
Tinicum
Timber Creek
Mantaes Hoeck el. Mantua
Swedesbogh
Christina
Christinas el. Minquas
Narraticons el. Raccoon Cr.
Nya Sveriges norra gräns enl. Printz köp 1649.
Fort Casimir
(N. Castle)
Sundhuk
Varckens Kil
Nya Sveriges norra gräns enl. F. Hollenders köp 1640.
Maurice River
Ellsborg
MARYLAND
NEW JERSEY
Appoquinimink
Nya Sveriges södra gräns
enl. Minuits köp 1638.
Back Cr.
DELAWARE
Murder Kil
Paradis Udden
Mispillion Cr.
Cap Mey
Zwanendal
De Vries's Fort
1631
Cap Henlopen
Nya Sveriges södra gräns enl. instrukt. för Printz 1642
KARTA
öfver
KOLONIEN NYA SVERIGE
(1638-1655)

Södermanland, came to the Delaware in 1641 from the prison at Smedjegården, close to the royal palace in Stockholm. He got into trouble shortly after his arrival, but later on he became a trusted member of the colony.

An equestrian (*ryttare*) by the name of Hans Månsson, from Skara in Skaraborg County, had been convicted of cutting down six apple trees and two cherry trees, the property of the Crown, from the garden of the old monastery church of Varnhem. He was sentenced to death by hanging, but this was commuted to deportation and he was sent to New Sweden. Arriving in 1641, he started his life there as a laborer. Very soon, he became a freeman, and finally, he became a captain in the British army, living until the 1690s. In 1975, a descendant of his, R.K. Turp, published the story of the family and its life in western New Jersey.

Another convict who came to the colony was Olof Stille of Penningby in Roslagen, Uppland, who was sentenced to death in 1638 for robbery. The sentence was commuted to a large fine. Although there seems to be no direct connection with the crime, Stille emigrated to the colony, arriving in New Sweden in 1641. Despite his dubious past, he made good in the colony, becoming a freeman and a millwright, and many of his descendants have attained prominent positions in society.

There was a rapid turnover of people in the colony. Many succumbed to disease. Others moved to Maryland and other areas outside New Sweden. In 1654, the population had sunk to 70, but the same year saw a strong increase, mainly due to the arrival of the ship *Örnen* ("The Eagle") which, despite a difficult

The colony of New Sweden after purchases and instructions, 1638, 1640, 1642, 1649. Many forts and places had Swedish names: Christina, Finland, Nya Göteborg, Upland, Mölndal, Wasa, Nya Korsholm, Elfsborg.

crossing due to a terrible disease on board, brought a few hundred new inhabitants to the colony. By the end of the year, the population had reached 370. The last expedition from the old country arrived in 1656, after the Dutch conquest of the colony. More than 100 arrived, mainly Värmland Finns.

In the early years, the colony was commanded by the military commander of Fort Christina, the most important of the fortifications in New Sweden. From 1643 onwards, the colony had an appointed Governor. The first was Johan Printz, of Bottnaryd in Jönköping County, who held the position until 1653. Printz tried in principle to have good relations with the Indians, but sometimes he became furious with them, and in 1644 he suggested a campaign to uproot them. However, this was not carried out. Eventually, many of the colonists came to regard him as a despot, and in 1653 a group of the leading inhabitants organized a protest against him. Several of them moved to Maryland, and Printz himself returned to Sweden. He was succeeded by Johan Rising, of Norrköping in Östergötland County, who restored order in the colony, whereupon several of those who had moved to Maryland returned.

By this time, external pressure on the Swedish colony was growing. The Dutch disliked the Swedish presence and, with greater resources than the Swedes, they conquered New Sweden in 1655. Their triumph was short-lived. In 1664, they were forced to yield to the British. However, neither Dutch nor British rule meant any change of ethnic character. The Swedes kept their settlements, and new groups arrived from the old country, for instance a group of Medelpad Finns, in the 1660s.

Although many of the newcomers (though not the majority) had Finnish as their mother-tongue, the Swedish language came to dominate, whereas Finnish seems to have disappeared after one or two generations. One reason for this was the activity of the clergy, who preached only in Swedish. Some Finns seem to have gone directly from using Finnish to using English.

Meeting between Swedish colonists and Indians. Engraving on copper by Thomas Campanius Holm, published in his work Kort Beskrifning om Provincien Nya Swerige uti America, *1702. Holm had not visited New Sweden himself but relied on descriptions made by his grandfather Johannes Campanius, who was pastor there from 1643 to 1648, and by the fortifications engineer Per Lindheström, who lived in the colony in 1654 and 1655. The picture intends to show the friendly attitude of the Swedes to the Indians as contrasted to the bitter internal feuding between the Indians.*

THE DESCENDANTS OF THE COLONISTS OF NEW SWEDEN

The colonists of New Sweden kept their Lutheran faith. From 1640 onwards, they had their own pastors, and from 1697 to the 1780s, Swedish clergymen were sent over to the four Swedish congregations, namely Christina in Delaware, Wicaco in Pennsylvania, Raccoon and Penn's Neck in New Jersey. Some of the Swedish churches, known as "Old Swedes", have been preserved. Though not Lutheran any more, the original Wicaco church, founded in Philadelphia in 1700 and now known as Gloria Dei Church, is the oldest used church in Pennsylvania. During the eighteenth century, some Swedes became Quakers, and between 1790 and 1831, the old Swedish congregations became successively incorporated into the Episcopalian Church.

In Sweden itself, the keeping of church registers was introduced during the seventeenth century, and this custom spread to the Swedish congregations on the Delaware. Consequently, the population of New Sweden is much better registered than are the populations of other groups in colonial America. Not only have abundant records of baptisms, marriages, and deaths been preserved, but also the counterparts of the parish catechetical-meeting registers (*husförhörslängder*) that had to be held by law in the old country. These documents contain not only biographical and genealogical information, but also, in many cases, notices about church activities, people's linguistic abilities, and the division between the English and the Swedish languages.

In 1697, one of the Swedish pastors noted that 1,200 inhabitants in the Delaware area spoke a Swedish as pure as that of the old country, although with elements of the dialects of Västergötland or Östergötland. To this number we must add the descendants of Swedish immigrants living in Maryland, New York, and other colonial states. At that time, there were about 2,000 Swedish-speaking Americans in the colonies, forming about 0.7 percent of the total population, which was 3 million. By 1900, there were 1.1 million first- or second-generation Swedes living in the United States, which meant 1.5 percent of the population. As far as absolute numbers are concerned, the difference is tremendous, but in percentage it is not very great.

In 1754, a census of the four Swedish congregations was made. Almost 1,300 members were recorded, not counting the children who could not read. The majority spoke Swedish and most of them could read English, while forty percent could also read Swedish. The area was now bilingual. Americanization was an inexorable process which seems to have accelerated after the War of Independence. However, the process was slower in the Swedish settlements than it would be during the period of mass emigration in the nineteenth and twentieth centuries, although those who left the New Sweden area and in many cases married Americans became Americanized more quickly — like the Swedes in the big cities during the second half of the nineteenth century. The process did not always mean ordinary Americanization — some Swedes married Indians and melted into an Indian environment.

The Swedish contribution to the general development of the area along the Delaware was extensive. Swedes were considered to be good farmers. William Penn, founder of the state of Pennsylvania, was highly appreciative of the Swedish presence. The Swedes excelled in such important crafts as milling, shipbuilding, sawmilling, and brickmaking. The most typical contribution is undoubtedly the log cabin, which spread successively westwards, partly as a consequence of migration. The Swedish origin of the log cabin has often been doubted and indeed repudiated, but modern research has proved it to be true.

Swedish missionary work among the native Indians was considerable, and the Indians were treated comparatively well by the Swedes. In the 1640s, the clergyman Johannes Campanius produced a dictionary of the Indian language spoken in the area, and later he translated Luther's catechism into the same

The Morton Homestead in Essington, Pennsylvania, is the oldest preserved example of a Scandinavian "pair cabin" (parstuga) in America, possibly from the end of the seventeenth century.

language. This translation was published in Stockholm in 1696, after the death of Campanius.

The number of descendants of the colonists of New Sweden has, of course, grown and must now be counted in hundreds of thousands, if not in millions. By now, the Swedish element of the ancestry is very slight, and quite unknown to some, even if surprisingly many are aware of it. One of the soldiers in the colony, Jöran Kyn — a contemporary register notes that he came from Saxony — had at least 465 descendants by the beginning of the nineteenth century. The family name is now spelled Keen, and one of the family, Dr. William W. Keen, who was born in Philadelphia in 1837, has been called "the father of

20

surgery in America". In 1907, to celebrate the bicentenary of the birth of Carl von Linné, he received an honorary degree in medicine at the University of Uppsala. Keen claimed himself that he drew strength from his "Viking blood".

Very few of those descended from the New Sweden colonists still retain Swedish surnames, although Mattson, Hendrickson, and Swanson can be found. Most of the names were anglicized during the first generations. Stille became Stillé, Stillman, or Steelman; Långåker became Longacre; Stålcofta became Stalcop or Stalcup (this name is still to be found at a farmers' market in Virginia); Bonde (not the noble Bonde) became Boon; Jonasson became Jones; Mårtensson became Morton; Joachimsson (from Schleswig-Holstein) became Yocom; Gustavsson became Justis; and so on.

Swedish or Finnish family names are sometimes to be found in place or street names. Dolbows Landing in New Jersey comes from Dalbo, which is probably from *Dalslänning,* one who comes from the province of Dalsland. Keans Lake and Mullica Hill in New Jersey; Longacre Boulevard, Matson Ford Road, and Morton Avenue in Pennsylvania; and Swansonville in Virginia, all have Swedish or Finnish etymology.

During the colonial period, the opportunities for social advancement were good. Several Swedish Americans who made the top can be mentioned.

The most prominent is John Hanson, one of the "great forefathers" of Maryland. His Swedish origins are not established beyond doubt. An Anders Hanson arrived in New Sweden in 1642, a farmhand who later became a freeman. One of his daughters, Katarina, was buried in 1646 in Tinicum, Pennsylvania, the first to be buried there. Anders Hanson took part in the action against Governor Printz in 1653 but then seems to have left for Maryland, where he died in 1655. Among his descendants have been many prominent citizens, and their Swedish origins are quite clear.

Other Hansons are mentioned in Maryland, too. A 1656 document mentions three brothers Hanson: William, Randolph, and John. The last-named was the grandfather of the famous John Hanson. A later quotation of the document (1876) explicitly names them as Swedes. According to a family tradition, they were brothers of Anders (Andrew) Hanson. The tradition also claims that the family originally moved from England to Sweden at the end of the sixteenth century. The name Randolph may be an indication of non-Swedish, perhaps English, ancestry. Some modern statements about this particular family are quite fictitious and should be regarded as family legend. One says that the man who emigrated from England to Sweden married an aristocratic Swedish lady – the most fantastic version gives her the name of Margareta Vasa, of the royal family of Vasa. She never existed, and neither did "Colonel John Hanson", said to have died at Lützen in 1632 together with his "relative" Gustavus Adolphus. Neither is there any foundation for the belief that the Hanson brothers were protected by Queen Christina and Governor Printz. It is, however, possible – and even probable – that John Hanson had some Swedish background, whether or not he belonged to the same family as Anders Hanson.

Another leading figure of the young American republic, John Morton, was undoubtedly of Swedish stock. One of the passengers on board *Örnen* in 1654 was Mårten Mårtensson. He died in 1706 and the funeral register notes that he was then regarded as being one hundred years old. According to the same source, he was born "in Finland in Sweden". Finland has, correctly, been described as a part of Sweden. Since the people on board *Örnen* were recruited in central Sweden, it is probable that Mårten Mårtensson was one of the many Finns who had settled there. Attempts have been made to localize his family to Österbotten in Finland but there is no evidence for this. His wife, Helena, who died in 1713 at the age of ninety-seven, was noted in the funeral register as being Swedish-born. Their son, Mårten Mårtensson Jr., was born in Sweden before they departed. The family name was changed to Mårten, Mårton, and finally Morton. Mårten Mårtensson Jr. was the grandfather of John Morton, who represented the State of Pennsylvania at the signing of the Declaration of Independence in 1776. It is said that his vote and signature were decisive for the position of the state and indirectly for the whole colonial area, since the votes were split on both levels. It can be added that the city of Philadelphia has the Swedish colors, blue and yellow, in its coat-of-arms. John Morton himself understood Swedish and married a woman from the Justis (Gustafsson) family, which came from Kinnekulle, in Skaraborg County. One of Morton's descendants, Dr. Howard McIlvain Morton, a well-known physician born in Philadelphia and living in Minneapolis, died in 1939.

Per Gunnarsson Rambo was one of the first colonists, arriving in 1640. His name has quite wrongly been connected with Rambo in Västerbotten, and he has also been said to be a native of Vasa in Österbotten. As a matter of fact, his grandson on the male side informed Pehr Kalm (the Swedish-Finnish scientist) during the latter's visit to New Jersey in 1749 that Rambo was a native of Stockholm, whereas a grandson on the maternal side said that his grandfather was from Västergötland and that the original family name was Ramberg. Since Rambo had a sister in Göteborg, the localization to Västergötland is the more probable one.[1] The village of Ramberg in Rölanda, Älvsborg County, *may* have been the original home. Rambo, who lived until 1698, became a highly respected member of the colony. He had numerous offspring, and the family still exists. A descendant on the female side was Harold L. Ickes, Secretary of State of the Interior under Franklin D. Roosevelt and Harry S. Truman.

Another of the 1640 arrivals was Sven Gunnarsson. His place of birth is unknown. A guess is that he was the brother of Per Gunnarsson Rambo, but that is unlikely. He came with his wife and at least two sons on the *Kalmar Nyckel* — one of the sons was actually born on board. Per Gunnarsson took part in the actions against Governor Printz in 1653 and 1654, but he stayed on in New Sweden, where he still lived in 1677. The sons called themselves Svensson, which later became Swanson. The most famous descendant was Claude A. Swanson, born in Swansonville, Virginia, who became governor of Virginia and later Secretary of the Navy under Franklin D. Roosevelt.

The artist Gustav Hesselius was born in Sweden and came to Pennsylvania in 1712. He has sometimes been called the first painter in America, and his son, John Hesselius, has been given the epithet "America's first native artist". Gustav Hesselius's portrait of the Indian chieftain Lapowian in 1735 is regarded as the first of its sort. Hesselius's granddaughter married another Swedish-born artist, Adolph Ulric Wertmüller, who painted a portrait of George Washington. James Fenimore Cooper, the writer famous for his Indian novels — among them *The Last of the Mohicans* (1825) — should also be mentioned in this context, as his mother had a Swedish background.

The feeling of their Swedishness is still alive among some of the descendants of the New Sweden colony, in the same way as the feeling of foreign ancestry has survived among some of the descendants of the Scots and Walloons who emigrated to Sweden in the seventeenth century. Swedish colonial societies have been founded in Wilmington and Philadelphia, and several organizations in Delaware, Pennsylvania, and New Jersey prepare themselves to celebrate 1988, which has been proclaimed "New Sweden Year" by the President and the Senate of the United States. A centre of this activity is the American Swedish Historical Museum in Philadelphia, the cornerstone of which was laid by Prince Gustaf Adolf in 1926 — the first member of the Swedish royal family to visit the United States. The building was designed by John A. Nyden, an architect born in Moheda in Kronoberg County. His idea was to combine seventeenth-cen-

The American Swedish Historical Museum in Philadelphia, erected in 1926. Both the architect, John A. Nyden, and the building contractor, E.P. Strandberg, were Swedish-born. The architecture is a combination of American colonial style and Swedish castle style from the seventeenth century (represented, for instance, by Eriksberg, Södermanland, which now belongs to the Bonde family).

tury Swedish castle architecture with American colonial style.

The history of the New Sweden Colony has been written by Amandus Johnson in two thick volumes published in 1911. He came to Minnesota in 1880 at the age of two in the company of maternal grandparents. Born in Långasjö in Kronoberg County, he was the son of an unmarried mother; his father was, at least according to Johnson, an aristocrat belonging to the old Swedish nobility. While studying, Johnson became fascinated by the fact that the poorer Swedish immigrants had, thanks to their countrymen on the Delaware, a glorious past in North America, of which he tried to make them aware. His research included archive studies in the United States and Sweden, and was inspired by both Swedish and American patriotism. He established the importance of the role played by Swedish Americans in the development of America, in its liberation from the British, and in the abolition of slavery. Some of the statements he made are quite untenable, but the research in archives was an important achievement and established beyond doubt the contribution made by the Swedish colonists and their descendants, despite their small numbers, to the history of the United States.

THE FIRST SWEDES IN NEW YORK CITY

Apart from the settlement on the Delaware, New Amsterdam, from 1664 known as New York, also saw an influx of Swedish immigrants. Although their number was small, perhaps just a few hundred, the Swedes left some traces, the most obvious of which is the naming of one of the city's most famous boroughs, the Bronx.

In 1639, Jonas Bronck, a sea captain in Danish service, arrived at New Amsterdam. One of his relatives, a seaman by the name of Peter Bronck, mentioned in the inventory of his property in 1643, was, according to a marriage certificate of 1645, from "Juncupping", which is the town or county of Jönköping in the province of Småland, Sweden. Swedish archives show that there was a family by the name of Brunck living in *Västra härad* in this county, so the conclusion must be that Jonas Bronck, who gave his name to the Bronx, was a Swede.

In New York City in the early days, there were plenty of opportunities for social advancement. One example of this is the

Hoffman family. Martin Hoffman, born in Reval, Estonia, which was then a Swedish province, arrived in New Amsterdam in 1657, where he obtained work as a saddler. He was regarded as a Swede. In 1733, his grandson, another Martin Hoffman, married Tryntje Benson, also of Swedish stock. Her great-grandfather Erik Bengtsson, or Dirck Benson in America, was born in Sweden and had arrived in New Amsterdam in 1648 via the Netherlands. Martin and Tryntje's daughter Cornelia was married to Isaac Roosevelt, who came from a Dutch family of patrician origins, and their descendant in the fifth generation was Franklin D. Roosevelt, President of the United States. President Roosevelt was aware of the Swedish element in his ancestry.

SWEDES IN THE AMERICAN WAR OF INDEPENDENCE

John Morton's role in the Declaration of Independence has already been mentioned and many descendants of Swedish colonists took part in the War of Independence in the 1770s. It is not known whether Swedish Americans also took part on the British side. More than 100 Swedish officers served in the French forces that supported the American side, and nearly 150 Swedes fought for the American or Dutch forces, but as far as can be ascertained, no contact took place between them and the inhabitants of the former New Sweden. The Swedish officers were more interested in the opportunities offered by the war than in the question of independence. A convinced monarchist such as Axel Fersen, who was a friend of Queen Marie Antoinette of France, had little sympathy for American demands for liberty from the British crown, even if he admired George Washington, but he took part in the campaign as an officer in the French army. Another aristocrat who fought on the American side was

Curt von Stedingk, a native of Swedish Pomerania. As a reward for his military achievements, he was made a member of the hereditary Cincinnati Society, and the head of the family still retains membership today.

The upheaval in America was soon observed in Sweden, and the poet Bengt Lidner wrote a dissertation on American liberty in 1777 and paid homage to George Washington in his poem "The Year 1783". King Gustaf III was naturally not enamored of rebellions against legal monarchs, but, at the same time, he was annoyed by the ruthless maritime policy of the British and was eager for the good opinion of France. So he allowed Swedish officers to go into French service, and, in 1783, he signed a friendship and commerce treaty with the United States. Sweden was thus the first neutral state to recognize the infant republic. In the following year, Sweden received the West Indian island of St. Bartholomew from France, and it became a rather important center of commerce with Europe. This colonial enterprise, however, was as little profitable as that on the Delaware, and in 1878, after a referendum in Sweden, the island was returned to France.

---

[1] As a matter of fact Rambo came from Hisingen in Västergötland outside Göteborg, probably in the neighbourhood of Ramberget. (Letter from P.S. Craig, Nov. 1987).

THE MASS EMIGRATION 1845 – 1929

THE SWEDISH BACKGROUND

During the first four decades of the nineteenth century, a few hundred Swedes — journalists, students, and military and naval men — went to North America. Of them, Sven (Svante) Magnus Swenson, a native of Barkeryd in Jönköping County, is perhaps the most interesting.

Swenson arrived in New York City in 1836. Two years later, he left for Texas, where he was to found a Swedish settlement with his uncle, Swante Palm, who arrived there in 1844. The settlement was near Austin, and most Swedish Americans in Texas are descended from the settlers. Many of them have good social positions in Texas and are conscious both of their Swedish background and of their place in American society.

Another Swedish pioneer was Carl Friman, from Varnhem in Skaraborg County, who was a military enrollment clerk. In 1838, he settled in southwestern Wisconsin, accompanied by his five sons.

In 1841, Gustaf Unonius, born in Finland but educated at Uppsala University, founded the town of New Upsala at Pine Lake in Wisconsin. He became a pastor in the Episcopalian Church but returned to Sweden in 1858, disappointed at the state of religion in the United States. Indeed, many Swedish dissenters, who were attracted by the freedom of religion in the United States, became disappointed, as it often turned out to be more a question of freedom from religion.

The real mass emigration began in the year 1845, when the farmer, builder and miller Peter Cassel, of Kisa in Östergötland, accompanied by about thirty people from the same area, founded a settlement by the name of New Sweden in Jefferson County, Iowa. The following year, the "prophet" Erik Jansson, a farmer and preacher from Biskopskulla in Uppland, founded a communistic colony in Henry County, Illinois. It was called Bishop Hill (the English translation of Biskopskulla); the members of the community came from Hälsingland, where Erik Jansson had lived prior to leaving. These so-called Jansonists (*erikjansare*) left Sweden because of animosity of the established Lutheran church to their sectarian and intolerant attitudes. The fertile soil of Illinois probably attracted them, too. In 1850, Erik Jansson was murdered by an enemy, and the colony broke up ten years later. But the town of Bishop Hill still remains, with its buildings typical of that time. Many of the farms in the area were founded by Swedes.

In the years between 1845 and 1854, the first stage of the mass-emigration era, about 15,000 Swedes emigrated to the United States, settling mainly in the Midwest, although a small number moved to California, attracted by the prospect of finding gold there. Quite a number of the Swedes were wealthy farmers and businessmen, interested in profiting from the opportunities available in the new country. The cholera epidemic that struck Chicago in 1854 slowed down the rate of emigration, as did the Civil War (1861 – 1865), but every year saw a small number of Swedes make the voyage across the Atlantic.

Apart from the Jansonists and some other small groups, such as the Baptists and, later on, the Mormons, very few Swedes left for America directly due to discontent with the established church. The majority of the emigrants were faithful Lutherans, and in 1860 a Scandinavian Lutheran Church, known as the Augustana Synod, was founded in North America. Originally Swedish-Norwegian, the Church became exclusively Swedish from 1869 onwards.

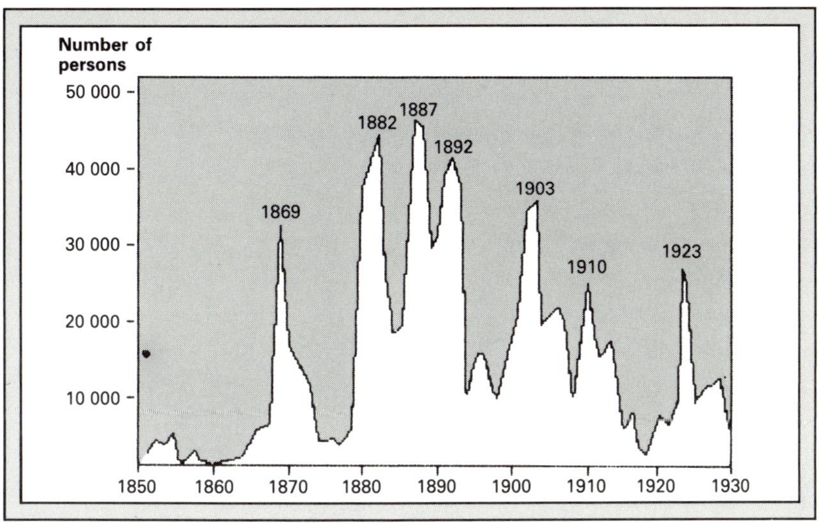

*Registered emigration from Sweden to non-European countries,
1851 – 1930.*

The next influx took place between 1868 and 1873, when crop failures caused a famine and over one hundred thousand Swedes emigrated to North America. The generous land legislation (the Homestead Act of 1862) attracted many farmers, who often brought their complete households with them. Many travelled alone, however, especially the sons and daughters of farmers, as well as maidservants and farmhands. By this time, there was regular steamship traffic across the Atlantic, and German and British shipping companies competed for passengers by advertising and through agencies. Accommodation aboard these ships was rudimentary, with little sanitation and other comforts available, and it was not unusual for the long crossings to claim victims.

During the 1870s, the industrial boom that took place in Sweden and the recession that swept North America caused a lull in emigration. By the end of the decade, though, Swedish agriculture and industry ran into fresh difficulties, causing an upswing in the rate of emigration. From 1879 to 1893, over half a million Swedes emigrated to North America, with young, single emigrants dominating the figures. However, a special category consisted mainly of married men who went on their own to America, leaving their wives (the "America widows") and children at home. Many such families were later reunited, either in Sweden or in America. In others, the husband sometimes vanished without trace, or the husband brought over some children to live in America while the wife remained at home with the other children, thus splitting the family permanently, although no legal separation was sought.

Increased prosperity between 1894 and 1900 again reduced the flow of emigrants, but without stopping it completely, and a new upswing came at the turn of the century. Between 1900 and 1913, over a quarter of a million Swedes arrived in North America. By this time, emigration was becoming a cause of major concern in Sweden. Previously, the authorities had consoled themselves and the nation by arguing that those who emigrated were more or less dispensable, because they suffered from a lack of patriotism, an over-adventurous disposition, or a deficient sense of duty. But in 1887, the poet Carl Snoilsky was uttering other thoughts: emigration was a stream of Swedish "heart blood" that ran westwards from "open wounds". By the turn of the century, the unease was spreading. Those who favored a strong army feared a lack of recruits, and farmers were becoming worried at the prospect of not finding enough labor. In 1907, the Commission on Emigration (*Emigrationsutredningen*) was appointed, but its recommendations came too late and did not strike at the causes of emigration. Above all, the agrarian factors — now less important than in the 1860s — were overestimated. For instance, it was assumed that young people would be kept in the country if some large estates were split up to provide small plots of land for families willing to work them.

"Emigrants from Orsa, Dalarna". Painting by Victor Helander,
1866. A young man takes farewell of his parents and other members
of the family. At the door, another emigrant is waiting for him,
fearing that the strong feelings may finally keep him at home.

World War I cut emigration to a minimum, but afterwards
the final upswing in the tide of emigration took place, peaking
in 1923 with twenty-five thousand emigrants. By the end of the
twenties, the American quota laws, the Depression, and the
expansion of Sweden's own industry put a definite end to the
era of mass emigration.

Between 1845 and 1930, about one and a quarter million
Swedes emigrated to North America. Of these, about two hundred thousand returned to Sweden before 1930. Every fourth or

fifth Swede born between 1840 and 1890 ended up in North America. Few other European countries were subject to such a loss of population through transatlantic emigration, the exceptions being the British Isles (especially Ireland), Norway, and possibly Iceland.

Most of the Swedes who emigrated were young men and women from the farming and industrial classes, with men somewhat in the majority. Maidservants, farm laborers, and the sons and daughters of farmers and crofters were strongly over-represented. After 1870, few farmers and crofters were found among the emigrants, the ownership of a plot of land, no matter how small, keeping them at home. The poorest of the country laborers, such as the *statare* (married farmhands who contracted to receive free lodging and most of their wages in kind), were poorly represented. They had families, little cash, and little of the adventurous spirit. The inmates of workhouses were also very rare among emigrants.

The industrial working class provided a high proportion of blacksmiths, especially before the great expansion of Swedish mechanical engineering at the end of the nineteenth century. Many tailors and seamstresses emigrated, too, as the prospects on the American labor market were better than at home. People with any sort of higher education were not inclined to emigrate, the exception being engineers. Entrepreneurs in industry, the trades, and commerce were normally not ready to leave their businesses. Civil servants, too, preferred to stay at home, even if government salaries were low. "The Crown's cake is small

Registered emigration to non-European countries from the Swedish län (counties), 1851 – 1930. The highest frequency is registered for Halland County — 5 percent of the total population emigrated per decade — as compared to Uppsala County, which had the lowest frequency, at 0.7 percent.

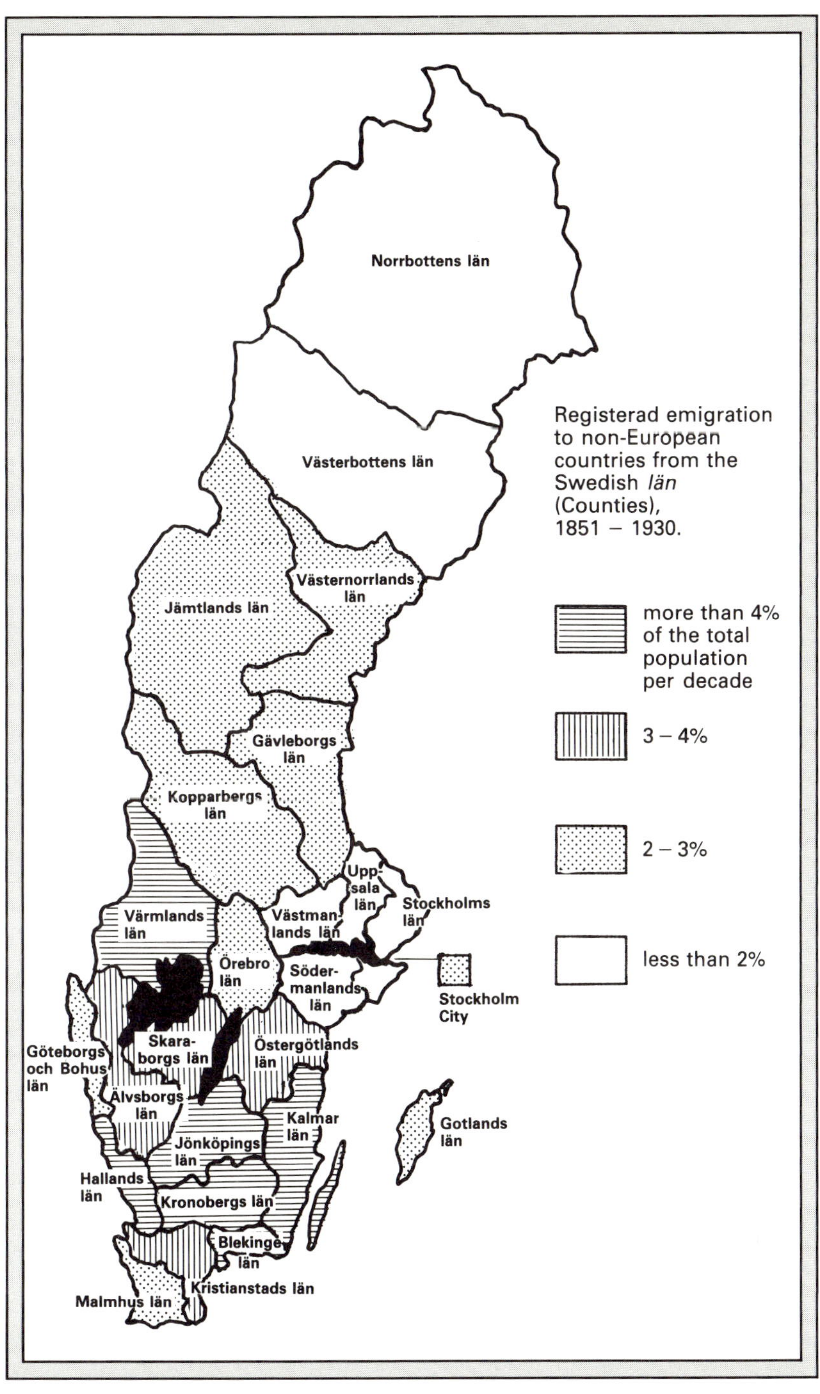

Norrbottens län
Västerbottens län
Västernorrlands län
Jämtlands län
Gävleborgs län
Kopparbergs län
Värmlands län
Västmanlands län
Upp-sala län
Stockholms län
Örebro län
Söder-manlands län
Stockholm City
Skara-borgs län
Östergötlands län
Göteborgs och Bohus län
Älvsborgs län
Kalmar län
Gotlands län
Jönköpings län
Hallands län
Kronobergs län
Blekinge län
Kristianstads län
Malmhus län
Registerad emigration to non-European countries from the Swedish län (Counties), 1851 − 1930.
more than 4% of the total population per decade
3 − 4%
2 − 3%
less than 2%

*The cottage at Bogölen, Ydre, Östergötland. Photographed by the
returned Swedish American, A.C. Hultgren, in 1915.*

but assured" was the saying. Even such lowly civil servants as
mailmen and station hands preferred the security of the home
country. Sailors and unemployed laborers were much more
prone to emigrate. So, too, were urban maidservants, whose
working conditions and status were far better in America.

On the whole, there was no general positive correlation between the degree of poverty and the frequency of emigration.
Young people were driven westward by the lack of security

available in the home country and by the prospects that lay before them in America. The strongest driving force was the surplus of vitality that arose in the overpopulated agricultural and industrial centers.

There was little difference in frequency between city and country dwellers among the emigrants. There was a clear geographic pattern as to their origins, however. The smallholder regions of southern and western Sweden — Småland, Halland, Öland, Dalsland, Värmland, and Västergötland — were all hard hit by emigration. Until the turn of the century, northern Norrland had very little emigration, as this part of Sweden was something of an America, for it offered many opportunities in agriculture, forestry, and mining. Throughout the period of mass emigration, the lowest frequency was from the country around Stockholm — Uppland, Södermanland, and Västmanland. Here, the rate of emigration was never more than a quarter of that in Halland, Småland, and Värmland. One of the main reasons for this was that those who wanted to change their lot would move into the city rather than embark on the long, costly, and dangerous journey to America. Indeed, many of those who did emigrate had often spent some disappointing years in the capital city.

The same was true for those who lived within reach of the provincial centers — Göteborg, Malmö, and Norrköping. A similar reluctance to emigrate could be seen abroad, in the surroundings of Copenhagen, Christiania (Oslo), Helsinki, St. Petersburg, and Budapest. In other areas, the "stock effect" was important: as soon as emigration had taken a foothold in a community or region, perhaps by accident, it often continued from decade to decade. The Swedish Americans enticed relatives and neighbors to join them in America; not seldom, they paid for the tickets.

Some of the emigrants returned to Sweden, usually after only a short stay in North America. A large part of them were farmers or sons of farmers, who had earned money in American forests, factories, and building enterprises before returning to buy a farm — often the paternal one. For their agrarian activities at home, the American experience did not mean very much. Yet within the mechanical and electrical industries, the furniture companies and rubber factories, such American impulses played a greater role.

The returning Swedish Americans also had an impact on the spiritual climate in Sweden, especially among Free Church groups (Baptists, Mormons, Pentecostalists, and so on) as well as on the Prohibition movement. The first Swedish Good Templar lodges in Sweden were founded in 1879 under strong American influence. The Swedish Temperance movement now changed from half-absolutism, mainly opposing strong liquors, to teetotalism.

THE SWEDES IN NORTH AMERICA
Fundamental Characteristics

Around 38 million immigrants arrived in the United States between 1820 and 1950, spanning three different periods. Until 1860, British and — to a lesser extent — German immigrants dominated the scene; from the 1840s, the Irish element was strong. British immigration continued in the second period until 1890, the Germans becoming ever more numerous; the Scandinavian share was by now significant. The Norwegians had begun to arrive in the 1820s, but the Swedes swept ahead of them in the 1870s, the Danish element being rather small. The third period, until 1930, saw a tremendous growth in immigration from southern and eastern Europe: Italians, Greeks, Serbians, Poles, Russians, and — among the latter two groups — Jews, who made a very important contribution. This new immigration, including an increasing Finnish element, was often regarded with disfavor by the earlier immigrant groups. Many Swedish Americans, who regarded themselves as a valuable and loyal part of the nation, now supported restrictions against the supposedly less desirable East and South Europeans.

The Scandinavians were assimilated into the American environment with relative ease. Their languages, except Finnish, largely resembled English, and the majority learned it rather quickly. However, the old Swedish dialects — undisturbed by changes in the Swedish language at home — survived for decades in typical Swedish settlements. And the linguistic change for Finnish-speaking immigrants has taken much longer.

Like most of the Protestant immigrants, nearly all Scandinavians were able to read. In Sweden, literacy was very high and the Lutheran reformation of the sixteenth century had created a strong interest in popular education. The clergymen encouraged reading to familiarize their parishioners with the Ten Commandments and the Lutheran Catechism, although writing was given lower priority. The demands on reading ability were enforced in the Church Law of 1686, and by the nineteenth century almost everyone was literate. This gave Swedes in America a great lead, compared for example with the Irish, Poles, and

───→

(Overleaf)

This picture from Långasjö, Kronoberg County, around 1900, reflects the typical Lutheran hierarchy in a Swedish parish. In the center the bishop, surrounded by earlier and present ministers and the teachers (including cantors) of the primary schools; pictures of the church, the school house, the vicarage, and the komministergård *(the assistant vicar's house). Many of the children in the schoolyard were future emigrants. Research by J. Johansson (himself a teacher) shows that the nonemigrants and those who eventually emigrated had about the same grades* (betyg) *in school, so as far as schooling was concerned, the emigrants were as good as those who stayed at home.*

Carlstedt

Rosengren

Leander

Elgqvist

Sjöstrand

Hjelmgren

Lå

Kantor Bergstrand

Skola

...kop Lindström

Linner

Sjöfors

Hörberg

Colléen

Kantor Lundell

...sjö

Kommenistergård

Skollärare Colleen

Italians. Moreover, the Swedish newspapers in America fed them with sound knowledge about their adopted country, even before they could read English. Reading helped them both to adjust to the New World and to maintain contact with their native homeland.

Beyond that, many Swedes had technological knowhow and skill. Here they differed somewhat from other Scandinavians. The Swedish farmers and crofters, usually living far from the commerce and handicraft of cities, needed to be self-reliant in providing themselves with houses and tools, and few were strangers to forestry. Thus it was not hard for Swedes coming from rural villages to take jobs at American building sites, saw-mills, and lumberyards. Metallurgical proficiency was well developed, too, especially among those from the district of Bergslagen in central Sweden, where mining tradition harks back to medieval times. Swedes often adapted easily to American technology, not least because the level of technical education in Sweden was high. A fair number of emigrants had certificates or degrees from technical schools and colleges, and this background was extremely valuable for their careers in America.

THE SWEDISH SETTLEMENTS IN NORTH AMERICA
Regional Distribution

According to the American census, Swedish-born inhabitants of the United States multiplied from 3,600 in 1850 to 97,000 in 1870, and to 478,000 in 1890. From then on, Swedes belonging to the second generation were also counted if they had two Swedish-born parents, or one American-born and one Swedish-born, or a Swedish-born father and a mother born outside Sweden. The only ones to be ignored were those who had a foreign-born father from elsewhere than Sweden, even if they had a Swedish-born mother. These were registered with the father's nationality. Within these limits, the entire "Swedish stock" embraced 776,000 inhabitants in 1890, making up 1.2 percent of the total population of the United States.

By far the strongest bastion of this stock was Minnesota, where it formed 12.6 percent of the people. Between 3 percent and 6 percent were registered for Utah, for North and South Dakota, Nebraska, Washington, Illinois, Montana, Wyoming, Colorado, and Idaho. In the south, with its hot climate, Swedes were almost nonexistent, less than 0.1 percent. Nine Midwestern states held 69 percent of the Swedish stock: Minnesota, Wisconsin, Michigan, Illinois, Iowa, Kansas, Nebraska, North and South Dakota. There were a further 17 percent in New England (from Connecticut northward) and the Midatlantic region (New York, New Jersey, Pennsylvania), 5 percent in the Mountain states (including Colorado and Utah), and 5 percent in the Pacific states (Washington, Oregon, California). Interestingly, many ethnic groups such as the Norwegians were still spread less widely than the Swedes.

The number of Swedish-born immigrants went on growing until 1910 (665,000), declining thereafter (to 595,000 in 1930). But since the second-generation Swedes were becoming more abundant, the total Swedish stock continued to increase. In 1930, it comprised 1,563,000 inhabitants, or 1.3 percent of the nation. Their regional distribution also changed a good deal between 1890 and 1930. Minnesota remained the most "Swedish" state, with 10.6 percent Swedes excluding the third and fourth generations. Washington now held second place (4.9 percent), followed by North Dakota, Nebraska, Illinois, South Dakota, Montana and Utah. The Midwestern part of the Swedish

(Overleaf)

Map of the Swedish-born in the United States, 1920,
and in Canada, 1921.

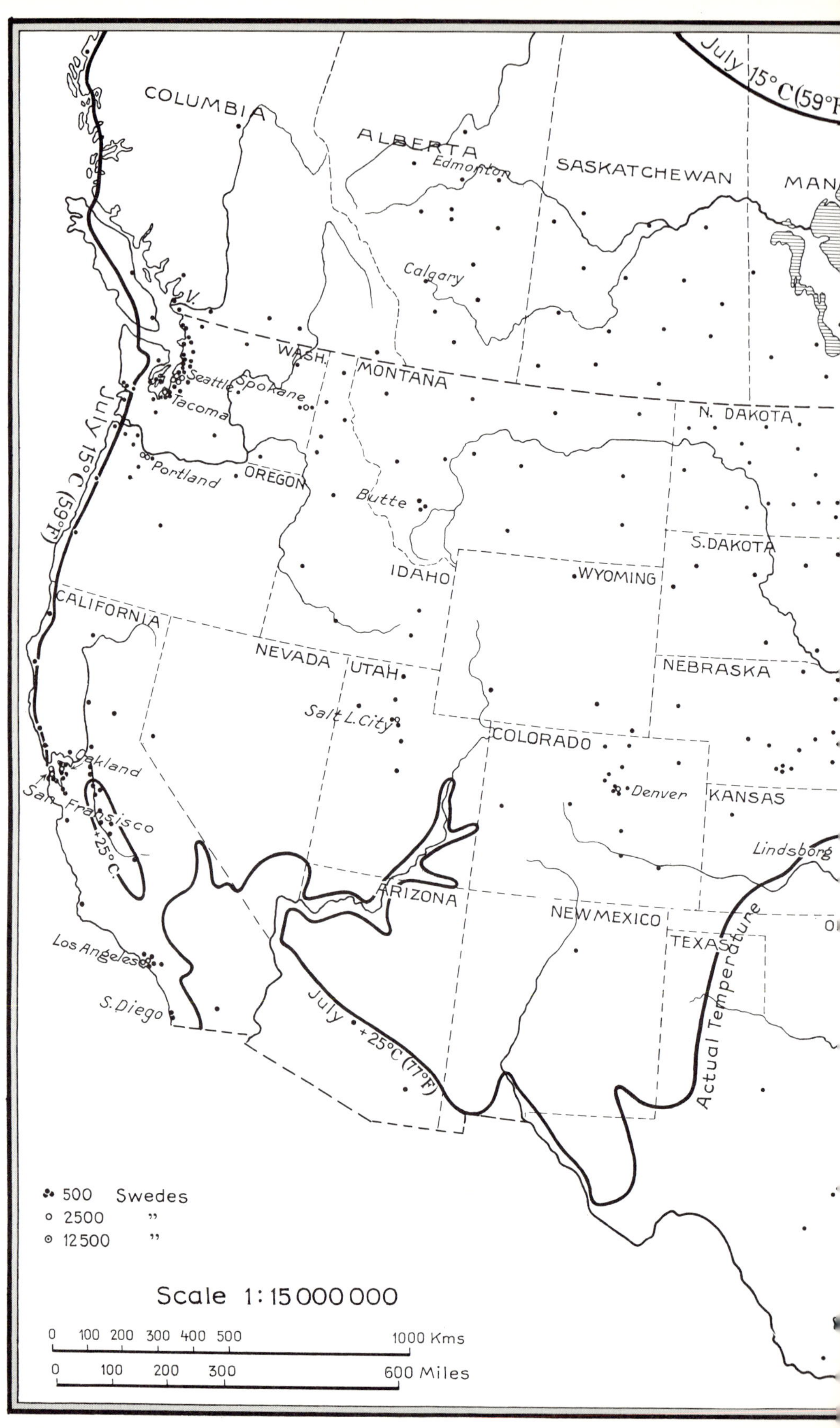

July 15°C (59°F)
COLUMBIA
ALBERTA
SASKATCHEWAN
MAN.
Edmonton
Calgary
V.
WASH.
MONTANA
Seattle Spokane
Tacoma
N. DAKOTA
Portland
OREGON
Butte
S. DAKOTA
July 15°C (59°F)
IDAHO
WYOMING
CALIFORNIA
NEVADA UTAH
NEBRASKA
Salt L. City
COLORADO
Oakland
Denver
KANSAS
San Francisco
+25° C.
Lindsborg
ARIZONA
Los Angeles
NEW MEXICO
Actual Temperature
TEXAS
S. Diego
July +25°C (77°F)
O
500   Swedes
2500   ”
12 500   ”
Scale 1 : 15 000 000
0   100 200 300 400 500   1000 Kms
0   100   200   300   600 Miles

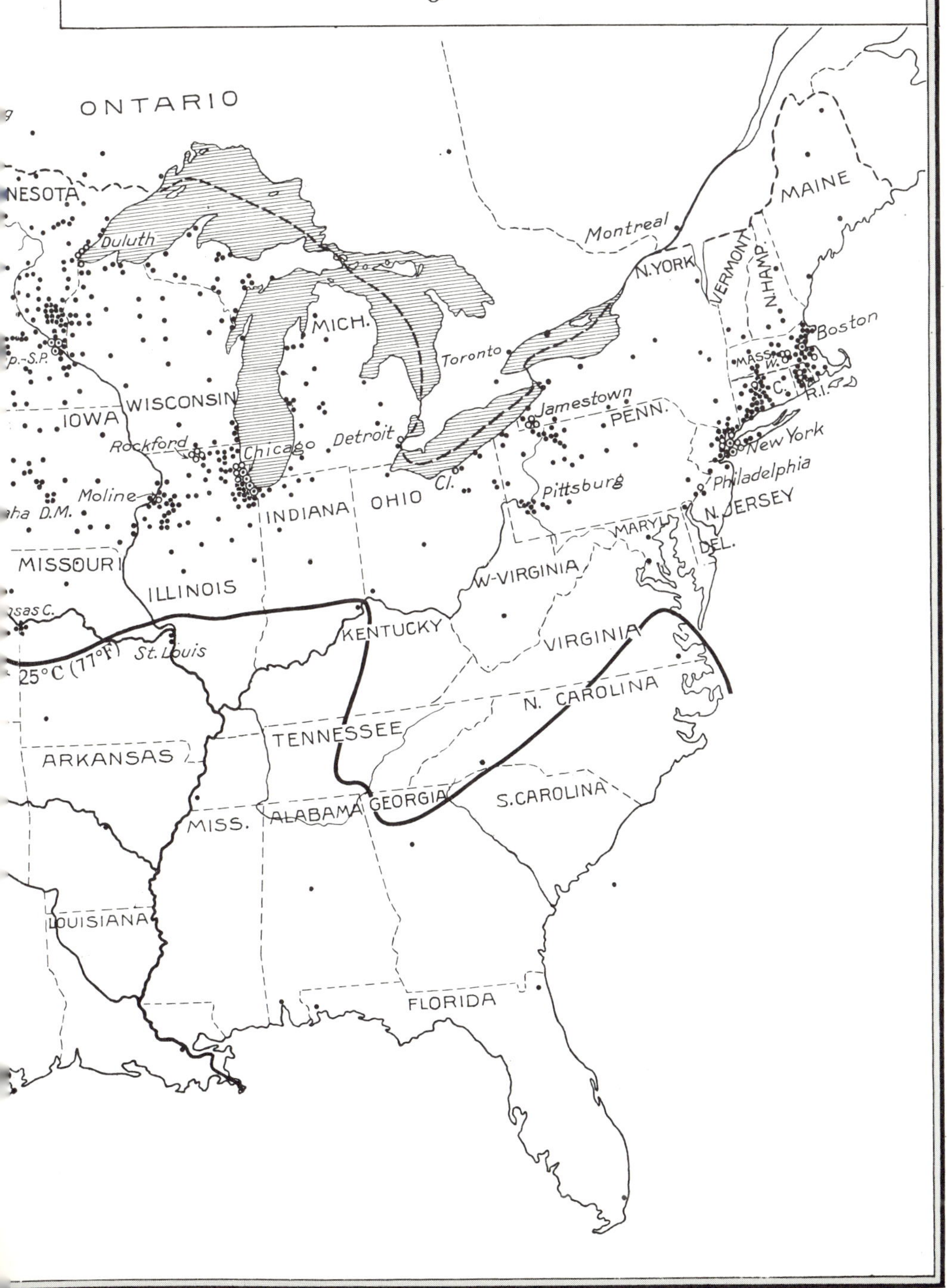
MAP OF
THE SWEDISH-BORN IN NORTH AMERICA
According to the Census of 1920 in the United States
and of 1921 in Canada
by
Helge Nelson
ONTARIO
NESOTA
Duluth
MAINE
Montreal
N.YORK
VERMONT
N.HAMP.
MICH.
Boston
Toronto
MASS.
W.O.
C.
R.I.
Jamestown
PENN.
WISCONSIN
IOWA
p.-S.P.
Rockford
Detroit
New York
Chicago
Cl.
Pittsburg
Philadelphia
Moline
INDIANA
OHIO
N. JERSEY
ha D.M.
MARYL.
DEL.
MISSOURI
W-VIRGINIA
ILLINOIS
sas C.
KENTUCKY
VIRGINIA
25°C (77°F)
St. Louis
N. CAROLINA
TENNESSEE
ARKANSAS
S.CAROLINA
MISS.
ALABAMA
GEORGIA
LOUISIANA
FLORIDA

stock had fallen to 54 percent, whereas New England and the Midatlantic states had raised their share to 22 percent, and the Pacific states to 13 percent. However, no change occurred in the Mountain states (5 percent) or the southern and southwestern states (2 percent).

Many Swedish immigrants were now attracted to the industries in Connecticut, Rhode Island, Massachusetts, and New York State. The westward movement expanded the Swedish element in California from 17,000 in 1890 to 104,000 in 1930, but it was largely a "secondary" process — the Swedish Americans, like others, commonly moved to the west coast from the Midwest. In California, for example, the settlement Youngstown was recruited heavily from Swedish Americans in Ohio and South Dakota, while that of San Joaquin Valley had a similar background. Some Swedes were also drawn to Alaska by its gold.

The Swedish settlements in Canada followed the same pattern. Before the 1880s, official Swedish statistics made no distinction between immigrants to Canada and to the United States. From 1881 until 1930, though, 18,500 Swedes were recorded as emigrants to Canada, most leaving in the 1920s. Indeed, the Canadian share was underestimated, for many emigrants registered as going to North America — or even to the United States — actually went to Canada. The Swedish stock in Canada totalled 81,000 in 1931. Most of these people lived in the western states: Manitoba, Saskatchewan, Alberta, and British Columbia. A great number had previously lived in states such as Minnesota south of the border.

Since 1930, Swedish Americans of the first two generations have become much fewer, whereas ever more inhabitants have a relatively distant, often mixed Swedish origin. In the census of 1980, Americans were required for the first time to register their "ancestry", either "one specific" or "multiple". A specific Swedish ancestry was reported by 1.3 million people, normally meaning that all their recent forebears were Swedish. Three million others had a "multiple" ancestry including a Swedish element. Further, 239,000 were exclusively "Scandinavian" and 236,000 had a multiple ancestry with a Scandinavian element, probably indicating a Swedish origin for at least half of them. Something like 200,000 Swedish Canadians are to be added, besides an unknown number of people who have some Swedish ancestry without knowing or mentioning the fact. In sum, the total of "Swedish Americans" in the widest sense must exceed 5 million, giving a Swedish ancestry to around 2 percent of the present population of the United States and Canada.

The Americans with a Swedish ancestry in the 1980 census are, statistically speaking, not quite comparable with the "Swedish stock" in 1930. Had the 1930 census included inhabitants with a distant Swedish ancestry, their geographical diffusion would presumably have been somewhat greater. Yet the difference cannot be large, and a direct comparison of 1930 with 1980 statistics will give a good picture of the general trends.

In 1980, Minnesota was still undoubtedly the most "Swedish" state in North America, 13 percent of its citizens having some Swedish ancestry. However, the relative number of Minnesotans with Norwegian ancestry grew from a slight minority among the Swedish-Norwegian stock in 1930 to a considerable majority in 1980 (712,000 against 528,000). This reflects the more rural habits of the Norwegians: they have not lived in big cities like Minneapolis as much as the Swedes, and thus migrate less often from the state.

Moreover, the highest number of Swedish Americans in 1980 belonged not to Minnesota, as in 1930, but to California (552,000) − although making only a modest part (2.3 percent) of that state's far larger population. In terms of Swedish percentage, Minnesota was followed in 1980 by Nebraska, Utah, North Dakota, Washington, Idaho, South Dakota, Montana, Oregon, Wyoming, and Iowa (ranging from 6.3 percent to 4.4

Långasjö skola, Chisago County, Minnesota, around 1910.

percent). Generally, the Midwest has lost much of its dominance, with 38 percent of the Swedish stock compared to 54 percent in 1930. The relative decline has been especially sharp in Illinois.

In New England and the Midatlantic states, too, the Swedish stock has given up ground (from 22 percent to 15 percent). Here, New York State has seen the biggest reduction. Apparently the old metropolitan areas do not attract Swedish Americans as strongly as before. The westward trend has also been very powerful, many Swedish Americans swelling the Pacific states (from 13 percent to 21 percent) and Mountain states (from 5 percent to 9 percent). Nor is the Swedish element in southern and southwestern states any longer insignificant, having grown from 2.4 percent to 10.7 percent, led by Texas and Florida, the latter a paradise for retired Americans. It embraced only 0.3

percent of the Swedish stock in 1930, yet 2.9 percent in 1980.

On the whole, Swedish Americans are now much more widespread than half a century ago. They can be found almost everywhere in North America, despite having lost some of their bastions in the traditional pioneer regions.

LOCAL LINKS BETWEEN SWEDEN AND NORTH AMERICA

The "stock effect" is an important factor for the Swedish settlements in North America. It means that many immigrants went to households and places where they could be with relatives and former neighbors. This effect may often have continued to operate for decades. Thus, some places or regions in America maintained special bonds with particular parishes or areas in Sweden.

An early example, mentioned already, was that of the Swedish settlements around Austin, Texas. Emigrants from Swante Swenson's home district of Nässjö in Jönköping County were rather dominant here. Another classic instance is the strong link between Långasjö, with adjacent parishes in Kronoberg County, and Chisago County in Minnesota. It was, in fact, so strong that one of the Chisago schools in 1915 was named *Långasjö skola*. Swedish dialects, especially from Småland, have survived there until the present day. For Vilhelm Moberg, himself born in this part of Kronoberg County, it became natural to stage his great immigrant epic (written 1949 – 59) in Chisago County, making that district well-known in Sweden.

A further Swedish county in Minnesota, Isanti, was recruited largely from Rättvik, Orsa, and other parishes near Lake Siljan in Dalarna, as well as from Norrland. The state's third typical Swedish county, Kanabec, had a more mixed background, with prominent elements from northern Sweden and

Skåne in the south. Its county seat, Mora, was named after Mora in Dalarna, probably due to a native of that parish. Here, a famous skiing event is arranged every year, emulating the great contest of the same name, *Vasaloppet*, at Mora in Sweden. A strong element from Skåne also existed in Washington County, where the first Swede in Minnesota – Jacob Fahlström – settled around 1844, having reached the territory already in 1819. Vasa township in Goodhue County was founded by a group of immigrants from Kristianstad County, led by the renowned agent, and later colonel, Hans Mattson.

Carver County in central Minnesota had firm connections with Älvsborg and Skaraborg Counties, while Wright and Meeker Counties were faithful to Fryksdalen in Värmland. Rosendale in Meeker County, however, was recruited mostly from Segerstad in Skaraborg County. Kandiyohi County received many settlers from parts of Skåne and Småland, besides Gagnef and Mockfjärd in Dalarna. The congregation Fahlun in Douglas County was largely settled by Dalecarlians. Ronneby in Benton County, and Borgholm in Mille Lacs County, were named after towns in Blekinge and Öland. In southern Minnesota, Sibley County was recruited partly from parishes south of Skara in Skaraborg County. One congregation in Lyon County took its name from *Vista härad* in Jönköping County. In Nicollet County, various communities were dominated by immigrants from Vetlanda in Jönköping County and from central Kristianstad County.

The Swedes in Wisconsin have tended to concentrate in the western part of the state, along the border with Minnesota. Pepin County was recruited mainly from Örebro County, and Burnett County from southern Dalarna, though also from adjacent districts in Bergslagen. Many of the Swedes in Michigan came from the lumber districts in northern Sweden.

Chicago was a very common destination for the Swedish emigrants. Some of them stayed only briefly but others became permanent residents. The Swedish stock amounted to 141,000 inhabitants in 1930, or 4.2 percent of the total population, a higher number than in any Swedish city at that time except Stockholm and Göteborg. Chicago received Swedes from all provinces. Before 1880, Jönköping and Kalmar Counties were somewhat overrepresented, at least in the congregations of Augustana and Mission Covenant. An unusually high proportion came from three *härader* in northern Småland: Norra Vedbo, Södra Vedbo and Tjust.

The area around Bishop Hill in Henry County, where the Jansonists settled, is the most typical rural Swedish district in Illinois. Here, some dialects of Hälsingland, Gästrikland, and Uppland have endured until our day. On the other hand, the most typical Swedish city in Illinois is Rockford, with a certain concentration of emigrants from Småland, Öland, and Västergötland. A district in Rockford has been called *Skaraborgs län*. Among smaller communities, one may mention Knoxville, whose early settlers came mostly from Blekinge and northern Skåne.

Iowa is a prairie state, with good agricultural conditions, but not ideal for those who liked to combine farming with forestry. The first Swedish settlers, the Cassel group, were from southern Östergötland and, to some extent, from northern Småland (Kalmar and Jönköping Counties). Boxholm in Östergötland has given its name to one of the small towns. Rather many of the Swedes came from Halland, after which another settlement was named. A few small communities have been dominated by immigrants from Kinneved in Skaraborg County and from Hultsjö in Jönköping County.

In Kansas, some small communities have strong Swedish elements — especially Lindsborg, perhaps the most "Swedish" town in America. In 1869, the clergyman Olof Olsson came to this area with 250 emigrants from Värmland. People from Järbo in Gästrikland settled around Enterprise, while Brandford has some traditions from Södermanland. A "Blekinge settlement" exists at Assaria, founded by immigrants from Jämshög. The community of Falun takes its name from the provincial seat of Kopparberg County in Dalarna.

Nebraska, with rich agricultural opportunities, seems to have attracted fairly many immigrants from Skåne, and one of the villages is called Malmö.

The two Dakota states have received far more Norwegians than Swedes, but the latter remain prominent. Highlands Church in South Dakota has been termed "Vederslöv Church in America", since a group of settlers came from Vederslöv in Kronoberg County. Clay County in southeastern South Dakota received numerous settlers from Rättvik in Dalarna.

In Colorado, the Swedish element is relatively small. The first settlement was Ryssby, founded in 1872 by immigrants from Ryssby in Kronoberg County.

The Mormon State of Utah is the most "Danish" of all states in America. Its Swedish population is also sizeable, and the emigration has continued since 1930 for religious reasons. Many of the Swedes have come from Skåne, a province with strong ties to Denmark.

The Swedes in the eastern states are distributed differently from their countrymen in the Midwest and Mountain states. A Swedish directory of Boston was published already in 1881, including much information about the origins of residents. It shows that more than 70 percent of the Swedes came from cities – especially Göteborg, Stockholm, and Helsingborg. The most Swedish community in Massachusetts was Worcester, recruited largely from either the pottery area around Höganäs in Malmöhus County, or from the mining districts in Örebro and Värmland Counties. The metal region in Connecticut drew Swedes from industrial communities such as Eskilstuna in Södermanland, Finspång in Östergötland, and Anderstorp in Jönköping County, the last having special links with Naugatuck in Connecticut. Some small communities in Pennsylvania should also be noticed: Wilcox, with immigrants from Halland; Irwin, recruited partly from Höganäs; and Arnot, with many settlers from Öland.

At the west coast, Washington State has the strongest Scandinavian element: Norwegians, Swedes, and Swedish-speaking immigrants from Finland. The Swedes often came by way of the Midwest and did not form close colonies. Swedish forest provinces seem to be overrepresented in this state: Jämtland, Ångermanland, Medelpad, Värmland, and Småland.

In California, the Swedish population is scattered, frequently coming from the Midwest. Many emigrants from Onsala in Halland went to San Francisco, thus moving from west coast to west coast. As a whole, Halland and Öland were apparently overrepresented in this state. For sailors and fishermen coming from Swedish coastal areas, California was a natural destination.

Canada, too, has scattered its Swedish inhabitants widely. The Sundsvall district was evidently overrepresented, especially in Manitoba. British Columbia has received many natives of Kronoberg County, as from Långasjö. In Saskatchewan and Alberta, an important role was played by the northern provinces of Jämtland, Härjedalen, and Västerbotten, besides Skåne and Småland in the south. A particular group was formed by the emigrants to Sweden in 1929 from Gammalsvenskby in the Ukraine: most of these stayed in Sweden, but some went on to Alberta.

In conclusion, our picture may look complicated, but there are distinctive features. The emigrants coming from cities and industrial communities were underrepresented in the Midwest, but overrepresented in the big cities, notably in eastern states. People from northern Sweden have shown some preference for northerly settlement — in Michigan, Washington, and Canada. Analogously, coastal groups were overrepresented in California and Pennsylvania. The typical agrarian emigrants, making up most of the Swedish stock, recruited to a very high degree the farming settlements in the Midwest, although many of them indeed went to Chicago, Rockford, Minneapolis, and other urban areas. Thus, the mass emigration played an essential role in the general process of industrialization and urbanization, which was going on in Sweden itself.

FARMERS

The vast majority of Swedish emigrants were natives of rural villages, and their longing for land was the main motive for emigration until the 1870s. For many, the dream of America meant a hope of putting their feet under a table they owned, and to harvest crops much more bounteous and valuable than what the narrow, parcelled Swedish farmsteads offered. In many cases, this dream was to come true. But the Swedes arrived generally later than, for instance, the Germans and Norwegians. They were consequently forced to go rather far westward.

In Wisconsin, except the westernmost counties, the Germans and Norwegians had already occupied large parts of the virgin country. Chances were a lot better in Minnesota. There the Swedes could combine agriculture and forestry in the same way as at home, although the vegetation was not very like that of areas such as Småland. The open prairie in Iowa and other states also attracted some Swedes, but frightened others. In the long run, the prairie held broader opportunities for farming than did the forest regions.

The rural midwestern districts became the residence for a hardy, ambitious Scandinavian stock which adapted well to the severe continental climate. Young families dominated the pioneer period. Women were scarce, and almost every girl who arrived was soon led to the altar of an Augustana pastor or Baptist preacher. The early marriages yielded many children, and unwedded children were extremely rare. At least formally, the Ten Commandments were observed.

In 1920, there were 60,000 Swedish-born farmers in the United States. Of these, 50,000 owned their farms, 600 were managers, and nearly 10,000 were tenants. Their cultivated land amounted to 11 million acres, including more than 6 million acres of improved land. The latter figure corresponded to over 2/3 of all the cultivated land in Sweden, which had to support more than 320,000 farmers and peasants, not counting crofters. Roughly speaking, an ordinary Swedish American farmer had over five times as much soil as his counterpart at home.

Vilhelm Moberg gave a vivid portrait, in his great epic, of the new opportunities for an immigrant farmer in Minnesota. The family, except the farmer's wife Kristina, adapted with considerable ease and success to the new surroundings. Sven Delblanc, himself born and brought up in Manitoba, presents a much gloomier description of North American life during the 1920s and 1930s in his partly autobiographical novel *Kanaans Land* (1984).

The proportion of farmers among the Swedish immigrants was quite limited, in comparison to the emigrants' occupations at home. In 1930, only about 20 percent of the Swedish American stock belonged to the rural agrarian population. Today, of course, this share is much smaller.

Their native country had accustomed Swedish-born farmers and wives in America to hard work in fields and cowsheds. This gave them a good start on the new land, but they had no advanced agrarian skills. Very few had any sort of agricultural education, and almost nobody was familiar with the problems of farming on a large scale. They had much to learn in America, even though they preserved some of the Swedish heritage. For instance, in Chisago and Kandiyohi Counties in Minnesota, the farmstead buildings were designed in the Swedish style with main rooms (*stugor*). In Chisago and Isanti Counties, the Swed-

Swedish American farmhouse, Michigan. The architecture shows an obvious Swedish influence.

ish-born farmers also followed Swedish tradition by keeping more sheep, and growing more oats, than did their American-born neighbors. Vilhelm Moberg's story of how Kristina planted Astrakhan apple-trees, with pips brought from Sweden, has a real parallel in Pennsylvania, where a daughter of Swedish immigrants was still cultivating, in the 1980s, peas that came originally from Halland.

In fact, Swedish farmers have made specific contributions to American agriculture. Sven Lindell of Jönköping County, and John Ferm of Värmland County, were real pioneers in the valley of the Smoky Hill River in Kansas. Peter Magnes of Jönköping County is regarded as the father of Colorado's sugar-beet industry and was also a pioneer of cattle-raising. C. G. Sjöstrand of

Kalmar County played a similar role in Iowa. The small area of New Sweden in Maine, founded in 1870 by the American diplomat William W. Thomas, was a large producer of grain, potato and animal products. Andrew Anderson of Malmöhus County, who owned a farm in Saskatchewan with tractors and sixty-two horses, received the very rare Master Gold Farmer Medal in 1932.

While these examples could be multiplied, it is nevertheless clear that the most characteristic and important Swedish contributions to American economic development are found in the industrial, not agrarian, sector.

ENGINEERS

Between 1850 and 1929, around 8,000 technical students graduated from Sweden's two leading colleges, the Technological Institute in Stockholm (*Kungliga teknologiska institutet* 1827 – 77, later *Kungliga tekniska högskolan*) and Chalmers Technical Institute in Göteborg. No less than about 1,100 of these engineers were employed for varying periods in North America, not counting travel for study. This proportion of 14 percent was greater than for any other group with higher education.

The emigrating engineers differed in important ways from the average emigrants. At least about half of them returned to Sweden, normally after a short time in North America, but occasionally after decades – an extremely high frequency of reimmigration. Many of the engineers did not go to America in order to start a new career. Often, their main aim was to acquire technological knowledge which could be useful for future activities in Sweden.

Another contrast lay in the pattern of destinations. Whereas only a fifth of the Swedish emigrants went to New England and the Midatlantic states, nearly 70 percent of the engineers went there, though some of them divided their enterprises between the East Coast and other parts of North America. Industrial centers in the Midwest, such as Chicago, Milwaukee, and Detroit, played a rather limited role. The same may be said of Seattle, San Francisco, and Los Angeles on the West Coast. Typical goals were Worcester and Boston in Massachusetts, New York City and Schenectady (an electrical center) in New York State, various places in New Jersey, and Pittsburgh and Philadelphia in Pennsylvania.

Their Swedish background, too, was special. Nearly half of the emigrating engineers had urban birthplaces, compared with about a fifth of the entire emigrant population. Stockholm and Göteborg were particularly overrepresented, whereas the opposite was true of typical rural emigrant districts in southern and western Götaland, as compared with the total stock.

Around a third of the engineers belonged to the mechanical and machine sector. Swedish American engineers constructed numerous machines, turbines, and instruments. A prominent example was Ivar Svedberg, born in Göteborg, who built some machines for working on iron and wood during his short visits to Boston, New York State, and Ohio. Another was Victor Hybinette, an expert in the production of nickel and its alloys. The son of a blacksmith in Falun (Dalarna) and descended from a Walloon family, he graduated from Chalmers and spent some years in Norway before joining the Orford Copper Company in New Jersey, then worked in different parts of North America as well as in Norway and Finland.

Emil Swenson, born in Denmark but raised in Varberg (Halland), also studied at Chalmers. He was employed by the Carnegie Company in Pittsburgh at the end of the nineteenth century, and constructed the first steel hopper-bottom freight car. Later, he designed the first steel skyscraper in New York City. Ture Rennerfelt, born in Värmland of a noble family, was active for some time in New York and New Jersey. He invented a vulcanized fiver collar, which proved very useful to the American Air Force during World War II.

One of the early Swedish engineers in America was Gustaf Jansson, born in Örebro County. He was not educated at either of the technological institutes mentioned above, but studied at a precursor, the famous School of Mining (*Bergsskolan*) in Filipstad. During four years in the 1870s at Washburn & Moen Company of Worcester, a company employing many Swedes, he introduced the "leaning floor", which became an important element of the rolling-train. Afterwards, he made a remarkable career at the Uddeholm Company in Värmland.

The second largest category among emigrating engineers, making up more than a quarter of them, was that of the electro-technicians. This branch sprouted in Sweden during the 1880s, dominated by the Asea company (*Allmänna svenska elektriska aktiebolaget*). At that time, the need for American impulses was great. One of the company's most capable engineers, Ernst Danielson, visited the United States in the early 1890s. While staying at the Thomson-Houston Electric Company (later General Electric) in Lynn, Massachusetts, he was impressed with the level of electrotechnical knowledge, the good administration, and the high tempo of work. Some years after that, the future managing director of Asea, Sigfrid Edström, worked in Pittsburgh, Cleveland (Ohio), and Schenectady. His visit was especially important for the electrification of Swedish street-cars. During the decades around 1900, nearly half of the emigrating Swedish engineers belonged to the electrotechnical category. Among those who stayed in North America, a native of Uppsala named Ernst Alexanderson became the most famous. In 1902, he was employed by the General Electric Company, and his inventions did particular service to radio broadcasting.

The engineers dealing with highways, canals, and bridges formed a third category. Here Swedish tradition was strong. A rather early representative in America was John E. Ericsson,

Ernst F.W. Alexanderson (1878 — 1975), born at Uppsala, the son of a professor in classics, educated at the Institute of Technology in Stockholm, came to America in 1901 and became a pioneer in radio broadcasting. In 1927, he gave the first home television demonstration in his house at Schenectady, New York State.

born in Stockholm County. He came to Chicago in 1884, modernized the water-supply system, and built some fifty bridges. Of a later generation was John Brunner, born in Halland, who built bridges for the city of Pittsburgh.

A fourth group were the chemical engineers, working in the traditions of the Swedish authorities Scheele and Berzelius. Emil F. Johnson, a native of Skaraborg County, came to New York City in 1887. As an analytical chemist operating his own business, he served there as public-health inspector, notably interested in milk control. He also arranged employment for Scan-

The encounter between the Merrimac *and the* Monitor *at Hampton Roads, Virginia, March 9, 1862, after a painting by J.O. Davidson, Library of Congress, Washington, D.C.*

dinavian immigrants. At the age of 83, he went back to Sweden.

Metallurgists were one of the smaller categories, exemplified by Emanuel Trotz from Stockholm County. He worked in Worcester around the turn of the century, becoming, among other things, chief metallurgist of the United States Steel Corporation, before returning to Sweden.

A fairly small, yet very significant, group consisted of shipbuilders. Among them was the most renowned of all Swedish American engineers, John Ericsson. He was born in Värmland in 1803, the son of a mine-overseer. Like many other prominent

Swedish American technicians and scientists, he descended from people who had worked as miners or metallurgists. His education was both military and technical, since no higher technical institute existed in Sweden during his youth. Becoming interested in railways, as well as steamboats, he joined in a famous locomotive contest in England in 1829. Among his many inventions was the ship propeller. In 1839, he came to New York City, where he died in 1889. The zenith of his career as a shipbuilder was the Civil War battle at Hampton Roads, Virginia, between his *Monitor* and the southern battleship *Merrimac*. The former's victory was a triumph for the North and gave Ericsson an international reputation.

Johan Wilhelm Nyström, or John William Nystrom, was of a younger generation. Born at Lofta, Kalmar County, in 1824, the son of a toolsmith, he was educated at the Technological Institute in Stockholm. In 1849, he reached Philadelphia, interested in both naval and railway transportation. Two books by him, published in the 1850s — about screw propellers and their engines, and on mechanics and engineering — contributed to the development of shipbuilding. He spent some time in Russia and Peru, but ended up in the United States after working in New Jersey, Washington D.C. (for the Department of the Navy), and Philadelphia. His reputation did not equal Ericsson's, but as a pioneer in engineering he was nearly as important.

The expansion of Swedish shipbuilding was deeply influenced by the American trends. A future managing director of Götaverken in Göteborg, Hugo Hammar, worked in the 1890s as a shipbuilder in Boston, Philadelphia, New York City, and Newport News, Virginia, partly for the American Navy. Ernst Hedén, belonging to the same Swedish company, was active in New Jersey and Massachusetts for some years after the turn of the century. John Lindstrom, born in Gästrikland, became a leading shipbuilder, businessman, and citizen in Aberdeen, Washington.

Two of the engineering categories were rooted in old Swedish mining — the distinct fields of *bergsvetenskap* (science of mining and metallurgy) and *gruvvetenskap* (science of mines). James Forsstedt, a native of Avesta in Dalarna, where his forefathers had been copper-masters since the seventeenth century, arrived at Worcester in 1880. He made improvements in the steel industry and took part in politics, earning the nickname of the "Swedish Demosthenes". Torsten Berg, born in Östergötland, the son of a schoolteacher and a younger brother of Fridtjuv Berg, the Minister of Education, introduced a long series of inventions and improvements as chief engineer at Andrew Carnegie's Homestead Mill in Pittsburgh. He returned to Sweden in 1902 as European representative of the United States Steel Corporation.

The smallest category educated at the technical institutes were the architects. Lars (Lawrence) Gustaf Hallberg, born in Älvsborg County, graduated from Chalmers and came in 1871 to Chicago, where he helped to build up the city after its great fire. John A. Nyden, a native of Kronoberg County, took part after the turn of the century in Chicago's construction industry with its many Swedish contractors. He has already been mentioned as the architect of the American Swedish Historical Museum in Philadelphia. In the 1920s, Illinois had about seventy authorized architects of Swedish descent.

The Swedish American engineers were a very successful and self-aware professional group, almost unparalleled among other Swedish emigrants. In 1888, some younger Swedish engineers in New York formed the American Society of Swedish Engineers, which still exists. Its first president was Carl J. Mellin of Skaraborg County, himself a prominent shipbuilder, working in Brooklyn for the Navy. One of his successors was Victor Hybinette. Similar societies were founded in Philadelphia and Chicago. The first president in Chicago (1908) was Henry Nyberg of Gotland, active in the automobile industry. Like a

*Advertisement for Aronsson's and Sundback's zipper,
printed in Paris around 1911.*

number of other leading Swedish American engineers, he had
been educated at an elementary technical school, in Malmö.

Indeed, the two most spectacular Swedish American inventions were made by engineers who had a rather special education. Early in our century, the foreman Peter Aronsson of
Örebro County and his son-in-law, the engineer Gideon Sund-
bäck (Sundback) of Jönköping County, educated at a German
polytechnical institute, tried to improve the zipper — a device
which dates back to the middle of the nineteenth century.
Aronsson did not manage to market his zipper, but in 1913
Sundback invented a system of lamellae which proved useful,
making its breakthrough during World War I. That was the
starting-point of the modern zipper. Sundback then began to
mass-produce it in Meadville, Pennsylvania.

The other striking Swedish American invention was due to

an American-born technologist of Swedish descent, Chester Carlson. He was born in 1906 in Seattle, but grew up in Riverside, California. His parents, both from southern Sweden, were crippled by illness, and he had to support them. For many years he worked in a cement factory but managed to finish his studies at the California Institute of Technology. During the late 1930s, while living in New York City, he invented the xerographic dry-copy process, which made him — after numerous difficulties — a multimillionaire. He died in 1968.

The zipper and the xerox-copy machine may stand as impressive symbols of Swedish American technological capability, shown not only by engineers but also by many employees and skilled workers.

TRANSPORT ACTIVITIES

Ethnic groups in the United States were depicted by the American author William Seabrook in a book of 1938. About the Scandinavians, he wrote for example: "They crossed the Atlantic, everybody knows, long before Columbus; then Lindbergh flew it first; and it's a fair guess, if they ever get to tinkering with the Goddard rocket, that they'll be the first to reach the moon."

This prophecy has, in a way, come true. One of the two first human beings on the moon, in 1969, was the astronaut Edwin E. Aldrin, a descendant of blacksmiths in Värmland.

Seabrook's statement is more than a mere curiosity. The Scandinavians, and especially Swedes, have made remarkable contributions to American development in controlling traffic at sea, by land, and in the air. Here their technological skill has celebrated its greatest triumphs. This is a consequence of Swedish geography: the long distances and the often difficult terrain made it urgent for the Swedes to solve their transport problems.

In the old society, communication by sea was paramount. Already during the War of Independence, several Swedish naval officers placed their experience and talent at the disposal of the French and, indirectly, of the Americans. An example is Baron Gustaf Rehbinder, born in Finland. He distinguished himself in an operation at Newport, Rhode Island, and was killed in action in the West Indies in 1782.

A signal achievement was made by Admiral John A. Dahlgren, born in Philadelphia to the Swedish-born consul for Sweden and Norway. As a boy, he was encouraged to study by Nicholas Collin, the last Swedish clergyman in the former New Sweden area. In 1843, Dahlgren moved from Philadelphia to Wilmington. As a naval officer, he introduced the rifling of guns and designed the first accurate gunsights. During the Civil War, he supported his friend Abraham Lincoln.

As we have seen, John Ericsson and John William Nystrom added much to American shipbuilding. The marine element among Swedish Americans has been strong even during the twentieth century. William Matson, born in Lysekil in Bohuslän, and originally a sailor, organized the Matson Navigation Company of San Francisco in 1901. It played a prominent role in trans-Pacific shipping, going to Hawaii, the Far East, and India. Many of the employees and sailors were of Swedish descent. The Swedish American Line, starting in 1915, was a result of cooperation between Swedes and Swedish Americans; its leader on the American side was Hilmer Lundbeck, born in Uppsala but living in the United States since boyhood.

A number of Swedish Americans have reached high positions in the American Navy. Captain George Fried, born in Worcester of parents from Kristianstad County, became famous after a rescue expedition in 1929. Later, he was supervising inspector in the Bureau of Navigation and Steamboat Inspection in New York. Rear Admiral Clarence E. Ekstrom, born in Wisconsin of Swedish parents, was in command of the Sixth

Fleet during World War II. Admiral Arleigh A. Burke, whose grandfather Anders P. Björkegren emigrated from Älvsborg County to Colorado, served after World War II as Chief of U.S. Naval Operations. Rear Admiral Charles E. Rosendahl, born in Chicago of Swedish parents, was a leading expert in lighter-than-air dirigibles, and took part in the sea battle of Guadalcanal in 1942. Rear Admiral Carl E. Anderson, born in Stockholm of a Swedish father and an Irish mother, participated with distinction in many landings on Pacific islands during World War II. He was regarded as "the world's champion beachmaster" and shouted in a jargon changing from English to Swedish "in direct proportion to the heat of his ready anger".

Although the major achievements of John Ericsson and John William Nystrom in the railroad industry were not made in North America, some Swedish Americans did become directly involved in the building of railways. For instance, P.P. Johnson and Martin Nelson worked at the end of the last century for the Oregon Company and other railway lines. Oscar W. Swenson, a native of Center City in Chisago County, Minnesota, took part in the development of Canadian railways.

Moreover, Swedes were active as laborers on the railways, especially in the Midwest. There, the workers comprised a special group, moving westward in gangs from site to site. Many of them later settled as farmers. The famous railroad builder James J. Hill, in a speech of 1902, emphasized the splendid revenue which his company was reaping annually from the Swedish and Norwegian settlements. According to a popular anecdote, he once said: "Give me Swedes, snuff and whiskey, and I'll build a railroad right through hell!"

One of the leading businessmen in Chicago, Bror G. Dahlberg, was born in Kristianstad and started his career as an elevator boy in Minneapolis. He learned the railroad business in Hill's company, the Great Northern. Another Swede, Carl J. Mellin, whom we have mentioned earlier, became a pioneer in

Charles Lindbergh and the Spirit of St. Louis.

the design and construction of advanced steam locomotives.

But the greatest Swedish name in American land transportation is Eric Wickman. He was born in Våmhus (Dalarna) in 1887, the son of a farmer. Some of his ancestors had sold hair products in St. Petersburg (Russia), Finland, and London. At the time of his birth, his father worked briefly as a lumberjack in Michigan. Eric took himself to Arizona in 1905, then moved to the mining districts in northern Minnesota. He was employed there as a diamond cutter and later worked in a car-hire firm. Observing that people had trouble in getting from their homes to their jobs, he arranged tours in his own car and then went on to procure busses. The activity grew fast, and its ultimate result was the gigantic Greyhound Corporation, which spans the continent. This company may be considered the largest of all Swedish American enterprises.

*Edwin E. Aldrin Jr., who piloted the Apollo 11 lunar module
which placed the first man on the moon, 1969.*

Many Swedes became engaged in the American automobile
industry. The most famous of them, Carl Edvard Johansson,
was born in 1864 at Fellingsbro, Örebro County, the son of a
farmer and sawmill foreman. During the 1880s, he worked as a
lumberjack in Minnesota and studied for one semester at Gustavus Adolphus College. Returning to Sweden, he visited a
technical Sunday-and-evening school in Eskilstuna. In 1910, he
started a company based on his inventions of instruments for
precision measurement. He was highly appreciated in the United States and, in 1919, he emigrated for the second time, to
work first in New York State and, later at Dearborn outside
Detroit, employed by Henry Ford in the mass production of
cars. In 1936, he returned to Sweden for the second time.

70

The big motor companies have benefited by numerous other Swedes, such as Oscar A. Lundin — the son of an immigrant from Kronoberg County — who has been vice president of the board of General Motors. In the 1930s, the managing director of General Motors in Stockholm was another Swedish American, Elis Hoglund, born in Chicago. His sons Peter and William Hoglund, the latter born in Stockholm, have reached top positions in the same company. They have good contacts with Sweden, notably with the car-makers Volvo. Many Swedish Americans have also been employed as engineers and skilled workers at motor companies in Detroit and other cities.

The Swedish contributions to the development of air traffic and the aircraft industry in North America have been striking. Erik H. Nelson, born in Stockholm, the son of an engineer, sailed to the United States in 1909, after study at the Technological Institute in Stockholm. He was first a rigger in a shipyard, then tested cars at a speedway on Long Island, New York. There he became interested in aviation and went to work in 1913 as a mechanic for an American aviator. Thus, he was active in transport by air as well as sea and land. In 1920, he served as engineering officer in the first flight from New York to Alaska and back, the only foreign-born member of the expedition. His great reputation was won by a flight in 1924 from Seattle via the North Pacific, Asia, Europe, Iceland, and Greenland, back to North America.

In 1928, Nelson joined the Boeing Aircraft Company of Seattle, then led by Philip G. Johnson, who was born in Seattle of parents from Värmland and Dalsland. Another pioneer of American aircraft was Hugo Sundstedt, born in Örebro. During World War II, he built transport planes of his own design.

No Swedish American aviator, and almost no Swedish American in any field, has equalled the fame of Charles A. Lindbergh Jr. He was born in Detroit in 1902, the son of a prominent lawyer and politician, and the grandson of a member of the Swedish Estate of Peasants, Ola Månsson of Kristianstad County, who was an eager participant in the railroad debates in the Swedish Parliament during the 1850s. Lindbergh grew up in Minnesota and entered the College of Engineering at the University of Wisconsin. After a few semesters, he left for the flying school of Nebraska Aircraft Corporation and, in 1924, enlisted in the U.S. Army Air Corps Training School in Texas. The next year saw him escape by parachute from a mid-air aircraft collision, which nobody had done before. In 1927, he took off from Long Island and crossed the Atlantic, reaching Paris after a day and a half. He was promoted to colonel, but left the Air Force Reserve in 1941, due to dissatisfaction with American foreign policy. Like his father during World War I, he was an isolationist. After the Japanese attack on Pearl Harbor, however, he supported the government as a civil expert in the War Department from 1942 to 1945.

Following Lindbergh, many Swedish Americans have done work in the aviation and aircraft business. One example is Edward E. Carlson, born at Tacoma in Washington State of Swedish-born parents. A career naval officer, he went on to become president and chief executive officer of United Airlines in 1970. Edwin E. Aldrin's landing on the moon in 1969 completes our survey of great Swedish American achievements in the transport sectors.

BUILDING CONTRACTORS

For an ordinary Swedish boy coming from a typical agrarian district without metallurgical or mining traditions, it could be difficult to adapt to the highly developed industrial environment in such American states as Massachusetts, Connecticut, New York, and Pennsylvania. But one nonagrarian sector lay wide open for the Swedish rural immigrants, as it had been already during the Delaware period: house-building. Even as youngsters, these immigrants had normally taken part in building houses on farmsteads, and in making wooden tools. So it was easy for them to take up jobs such as carpentry in Chicago, Minneapolis, and other cities. Some of them later advanced to become building contractors, not seldom on a large scale.

It took time to reach the top. In Chicago, the center of Swedish American building activities, a pioneer was Andrew Lanquist, born at Ving in Västergötland. Starting as a practical engineer on the Swedish State Railways, he came to Chicago in 1881 and took up bricklaying. In 1891, he erected the city's first real skyscraper. His company later produced many other tall buildings in Chicago, Gary (Indiana), and elsewhere.

In 1882, Henry Ericsson, a native of Moheda in Kronoberg County, moved to Chicago from New York State. His father, a farmer who had owned a blast-furnace, followed two years later with the rest of the family, and settled down to farm in Minnesota. Henry had studied at a technical school in Stockholm, and worked briefly in Chicago as a carpenter before becoming associated with Lanquist. From 1897 on, he was his own master. His younger brother, John Ericsson, beginning as a bricklayer, also became a prominent building contractor in Chicago, cooperating for a time with Henry.

Among many other examples of successful Swedish builders in Chicago was Eric P. Strandberg. A native of Jämtland, he arrived in 1882 and was to specialize in hospitals and other institutional buildings. One of his constructions was the American Swedish Historical Museum in Philadelphia. Louis M. Nelson, from Sunne in Värmland, arrived in the same year as a young boy and was especially active in Chicago's suburbs. Nils Persson Severin, from Skåne, came in 1888 and erected a number of private houses, churches, and official buildings, also in other cities. He supervised the remodelling of the White House in Washington, D.C., in 1927. Charles Boström, born in Värmland, came to Michigan in 1891 as a carpenter, later building private houses and industrial plants in Chicago. Eric E. Skoglund, born in Närke, arrived in 1897 as a stone-cutter like his father and went on to put up banks, hotels, and other edifices in Chicago. Adolph Lindstrom, of Värsås in Skaraborg County, came in 1901 and constructed apartments, hotels, business buildings, and the new Chicago Daily News building. It has been estimated that one third of the houses in Chicago around 1930 were erected by Swedish companies.

A later house-builder of note in Chicago was Ragnar Benson, born at Virestad in Kronoberg County. After World War II, he arranged extensive air travel to Sweden for his relatives, friends, and employees. Swedish contractors have also been very active in Minneapolis and St. Paul, although their companies seem to have been smaller than their Chicago counterparts. A leading role has been played in recent times by Axel H. Ohman, whose ancestors lived at Leksand in Dalarna.

Godfrey G. Swenson of Vimmerby, Kalmar County, came in 1896 to Kansas City, Missouri, starting as a stonemason. He progressed from journeyman, foreman, and subcontractor to become a big building contractor. Frank Anderson, a native of Ryssby in Kronoberg County, came in 1882 to Denver, Colorado, where he later erected the city's first eight-story building. There, too, Arvid Olsson of Kävlinge in Malmöhus County, arriving in 1888 after two years in Minnesota, built the Denver Auditorium and St. John's Cathedral.

In San Francisco, the earthquake and fire of 1906 created a huge market for building companies. Some Swedish firms took important roles. Numerous buildings were raised by Petterson & Person, whose leaders were Gottfrid Petterson of Älghult, Kronoberg County, and S. Persson of Ivetofta, Kristianstad County, both arriving in the 1880s. At the same time came Jonathan Andersson of Bärby, Västergötland; like the former company, he built blocks and town sections.

*Swedish Covenant Home of Mercy, Chicago, the new building
that was dedicated in 1927. The architect was
the Swedish-born John A. Nyden.*

The Swedish American building contractors formed a very
characteristic group during the period of mass emigration.
Their background was rather different from that of engineers.
Far more rural, they normally had less theoretical education and
were born mainly in the typical agrarian emigrant districts of
southern and western Sweden.

BIG BUSINESSMEN

As already mentioned, technical skill and education were an
important basis of early Swedish success in the United States.
Financial and administrative talents were less significant, and
very few Swedes of the first generation reached the financial top
in American society. One exception was Charles A. Smith, the

son of an infantry soldier in Östergötland, who accompanied him to Minneapolis in 1867. In 1878, he started a lumberyard in western Minnesota and was later regarded as one of the "lumber kings" of the Midwest. Most of his employees were Swedes.

A combination of technical and administrative capabilities laid the foundation for the Norton Company in Worcester, Massachusetts. It was started in 1885 by Swen Pulson (Paulson) and his brother-in-law John Jeppsson, both from the pottery district of Höganäs in Malmöhus County. Their company became the world's largest maker of grinding machinery.

Another sizeable firm was founded by John W. Nordstrom, born in Nederluleå, Norrbotten County, the son of a small farmer who was also a blacksmith and wagonmaker. In 1887, John went to Michigan, where he had a cousin. After trying various occupations, he travelled in 1897 to the Klondike in Alaska and discovered some gold. In 1900, he became part-owner of a shoe business in Seattle, beginning a family firm. It is now run by the third generation and includes a very large chain of stores.

The bank business has attracted many Swedish Americans, mostly educated in America. A Swedish-born pioneer was Charles John Ericson, from Södra Vi in Kalmar County. He reached Moline, Illinois, in 1852 with his parents and, in 1905, became president of the First National Bank in Boone, Iowa. Born in Sweden but educated in America was Edgar L. Mattson, a son of the famous Colonel Hans Mattson. He became president of the Midland National Bank and Trust Company in Minneapolis. Hugo A. Anderson, born in Helsingborg but taken to America a year later, began his career in 1901 as a page at the First National Bank of Chicago, where he finally became president. His son Robert O. Anderson, born in Chicago, became board chairman of the Atlantic Richfield Company in Philadelphia and has been very active in the oil business, maintaining many Swedish contacts.

A banking career also fell to Rudolph (Rudy) Peterson, born in 1904 at Svenljunga, Älvsborg County. He came at the age of one to his aunt and uncle in Ohio, then grew up in a Swedish rural community at Turlock in San Joaquin Valley, California, studying later at the University of California in Berkeley. In 1963, he took over as president and chief executive officer of the Bank of America.

Every visitor to the United States sees the name of Walgreen shining from neon signs at drugstores. Charles R. Walgreen grew up on a farm near Galesburg, Illinois; his father had come to America in 1852. After starting as a shoe-worker, Walgreen opened a drugstore in Chicago in 1901. In 1939, his son took over the management of a chain including over five hundred stores in thirty-one states.

The wealthiest Swedish American today is probably Curtis L. Carlson, born in Minnesota in 1914. His father, from Kronoberg County, came to that state as a young boy with his own parents and settled on a farm in Chisago County. Curtis graduated from the University of Minnesota and sold soap for a firm in Minneapolis. On Saturdays, he began to sell coupons — Gold Bond Stamps — to the customers. Despite many difficulties during World War II, he expanded in business, and now Carlson Companies is running hotels, restaurants, and travel agencies. The richest citizen of Minnesota, he plays a leading role in Swedish American activities. Unlike many of his counterparts in Sweden, Carlson does not avoid talking about his large fortune. It is, in his eyes, a proof that he has satisfied his customers.

Among the younger Swedish Americans active in big business, Rand V. Araskog may be mentioned. He was born in 1932 on a dairy farm in Minnesota, the grandson of a farmer from Araskoga in Malmöhus County, who eventually became a tax commissioner. After a military education and service in the C.I.A., Araskog went into business and is now chairman of the International Telephone and Telegraph Corporation, the world's largest industrial concern. Its operations include tele-communications, engineering, forest products, the Sheraton hotels, and insurance companies.

Evidently the Swedish Americans, in relation to their share of the American population, are or have been overrepresented within the technological, transport, and construction sectors. Whether the same is true in big business seems less clear, but they have certainly been successful in terms of big money. Their strong technological abilities have contributed to a number of "success stories". They have relied mostly on themselves — even more so than their counterparts in the old country.

Rudolph Peterson and Curtis Carlson were interviewed by Swedish television reporter Lasse Holmqvist some years ago, and were asked which American president they ranked as the best during their lifetime. Both answered: Eisenhower. He was excellent in their opinion because he gave his orders every morning and then went out to play golf. He and his administration were appreciated since they did not interfere in business life.

METALWORKERS, CARPENTERS, AND CABINET-MAKERS

In 1900, 33 percent of the active male population belonging to the Swedish stock in the United States were occupied in agriculture, 35 percent were in industry, and 14 percent in business and communication, while 16 percent were classified as servants and day-laborers. Less than 2 percent had "free occupations", mainly with advanced education. The vast majority of the industrial population, many of those registered under business and communication, and probably around half of the servants and day-laborers, could be regarded as nonagricultural workers, amounting to the majority of the Swedish stock. In Sweden

*Factory of Dahlstrom Metallic Door Company, Jamestown,
New York State. Charles P. Dahlstrom, a native of Gotland,
built the first fireproof metal door. In the 1930s, the company
delivered more than fifty thousand such doors to the
Rockefeller Center buildings in New York City.*

itself, the corresponding groups (*arbetarklassen*) included only a third of the active population. During the following decades, these proportions grew in both countries. Nowadays, however, the number of employees in service sectors is expanding most rapidly.

It must be remembered that the nonagrarian working class has always been more predominant among the Swedish Americans than among Swedes at home. The structure of this social class has been somewhat similar in the two countries. More than half of the male industrial Swedish American workers in 1900 belonged to the iron or wood sectors: blacksmiths, steel and metal workers, carpenters, cabinet-makers, sawmill workers, and so on. Typical American sectors, such as the oil industry and the coal mines, were underrepresented among the Swedish Americans.

Among the trades groups, the Swedish Americans seem to have been overrepresented as tailors, painters, and shoemakers, and probably also in some smaller groups like photographers

A gang of workmen with many Swedes at an American steel plant at the turn of the century. The picture was taken home to Sweden by Gunnar Oscarsson, Södra Sandsjö, Kronoberg County.

and undertakers. Yet they appear underrepresented as, for example, bakers, butchers, brewers, and bookbinders.

Many workers of Swedish descent were employed in companies led by Swedes. In Chicago, with its numerous masons and carpenters of Swedish descent, one single contractor — Adolph Lindstrom — is said to have sometimes employed about ten thousand Swedish-born workers. The metal and textile industries also had a strong Swedish element. In Moline, Illinois, more than one thousand Swedes worked during the 1880s in

Residences in Swede Town, Chicago, about 1880.

Deere's Plow Works and the Moline Plow Company. In some departments only Swedish was spoken. Swedish entrepreneurs and workers in Rockford, Illinois, were fairly dominant in both the furniture manufacturing and machine industries. Many Swedes, too, were cabinet-makers. A similar structure existed in Jamestown, New York. In Worcester, Massachusetts, the most typical Swedish branch was pottery. As late as 1914, up to 75 percent of the workers at the Norton Company were of Swedish descent. The steel industry in this city also attracted numerous Swedish engineers and workers.

The urban Swedish settlements were less homogeneous than

the typical rural ones, but some characteristics are noteworthy. Their biggest concentration was in Chicago. During the 1880s, more than half of the Chicago Swedes lived in "Swede Town", north of the Chicago River. One of the streets in this area, Chicago Avenue, was sometimes called Swedish Peasant Street (*Svenska Bondegatan*), a name which suited its rather rural and primitive looks. The low, simple houses or cottages were mostly of wood and lacked sanitary facilities. Often, two or more families lived together in houses intended for one family. The overwhelming majority rented their homes. But the ethnic structure began to change at the end of the last century: many Swedes moved to more comfortable parts of the city, while Sicilians and other newcomers moved in. During the transitional period, Swedish as well as Irish boys often fought against Italian youngsters.

Swede Town was gradually transformed into Little Sicily. Later on, the Italians were replaced by black people from the American South and by Puerto Ricans. A new Swedish concentration, although not as strong as the earlier one, arose in Lake View — including the present Andersonville. Here, the Svithiod Singing Club, Swedish Engineers' Society, and other clubs were established. But this settlement, too, was fairly short-lived. After some decades, many Swedes moved to suburban districts, mainly in the north. Every move meant a weakening of ethnic homogeneity and an increase in marriages outside the ethnic group. At the same time, these changes were a result of improved conditions for the Swedish worker population, and of greater social mobility from blue collar to white collar.

MAIDSERVANTS AND SEAMSTRESSES

Women were a minority, little more than 40 percent, of the Swedish emigrants to North America. Most of the female emigrants were young and unmarried; due to a shortage of women in the rural settlements, they could easily find partners within their own ethnic group. In the first generation, not many of them married non-Swedes, and extremely few married non-Scandinavians.

In the cities, however, young girls were often more numerous than young men, and a lot of women remained single for much or all of their lives. Often, they had to support themselves outside the family: in 1900, of the active women (excluding housewives) belonging to the Swedish stock, 56 percent were servants or waitresses, and 13 percent worked as seamstresses or laundresses. Smaller groups were the day-laborers and factory workers, and still fewer went into business, communication, agriculture, or "free occupations". This situation changed radically in the following decades. The share of maidservants decreased, while a growing part of the female Swedish population worked as clerks, typists, stenographers, and saleswomen.

The maidservants were the largest group in the first generation. In 1880, around 10 percent of the female domestic servants in Chicago were Swedish. For those who had worked in Sweden as maidservants, or as "home daughters" in poor rural or urban families, emigration meant an improvement. In America maidservants' salaries were higher, the lodging less uncomfortable, the workdays shorter, and the status better. Servants were often treated as members of the family, which was not very common in Sweden.

The clothes changed as well: in Sweden an ordinary rural girl could not wear a hat without being accused of vanity, yet in America hats were entirely acceptable. "You could have gone with hat and gloves among stylish American women," says Mr. Johansson, a former journeyman tailor, in a popular poem by Gustaf Fröding in 1891. This emigrant is thinking bitterly about his Swedish fiancée, who preferred to stay in Sweden and, consequently, was kept on a proletarian level. Such complaints

*Farewell in Göteborg. The girls were probably going to
Chicago for jobs as maidservants.*

about unfaithful partners are a common theme in Swedish emigrant poetry.

In Chicago, for instance, the Swedish maidservants were localized differently from most of the early immigrants. Whereas the families — and the young men — lived together in Swede Town, the maids spread out over the city and were employed in non-Swedish families, not seldom in very wealthy households which also had nursery maids: Swedish nursery maids seem to have retained a good reputation. The result was a high percentage of marriages outside the Swedish population.

In the industrial sector, the seamstresses and "sewing girls" constituted the largest group. In Chicago, the Swedish part of the female labor force in 1880 was around 6 percent in the textile industry. Single seamstresses were employed mainly by sewing factories, whereas many housewives worked at home with their borrow- and sewing-machines by contract with various employers. Some of these women sewed buttonholes, or tacked and stitched, under uncertain and unfavorable conditions. Normally, they had a good training from their Swedish homes, which had taught them to deal with needle and thread.

Some of the Swedish female immigrants worked in laundries; a few started their own laundry businesses. In St. Peter, Minnesota, Christina Johnson, born in Östergötland and married to a Swedish blacksmith who ended up in the poorhouse, supported herself and her son — the future Governor John A. Johnson — by going from family to family, taking care of the laundry.

A small minority of all these women managed to advance socially through their marriages or, like Christina Johnson, through their children. Extremely few could reach high positions by their own effort. An example was Mary Anderson, born on a tiny farm in Skaraborg County. For many years, she worked as a stitcher and shoe repairer in Chicago. She joined a trade union and was employed by the International Boot and Shoe Workers' Union. After World War II, she became director of the Women's Bureau of the U.S. Department of Labor.

THOSE WHO DISAPPEARED

As has already been explained, the main purpose of this study is to emphasize the typical Swedish contributions to American technical, cultural, and political development. This means, of course, that socially successful biographies and destinies are highlighted. Those who have fully or partially realized the "American dream", on lofty or moderate levels, have naturally influenced their contemporaries – and the whole American way of life – far more than did those who have failed or faded from view.

The latter immigrants remain more or less anonymous. They wrote no letters or autobiographies, and their names cannot be found in the local chronicles. Yet they, too, are a part of Swedish American history. When we try to restore their rightful place, we must also remember that all history contains an element of failure. Equally among the Swedes who stayed at home, there were numerous catastrophes, bankruptcies, suicides, and crimes. The difference is that such fates are better recorded in Sweden than America, or at least easier to follow. The risk of total disappearance and oblivion was greater in America than at home. The question is: to what degree did emigration itself create utter failures, personal breakdowns, and disappearances?

This cannot be answered with exact statistics, but several observations may be made. The best material is provided by a study of emigrants from Långasjö in Kronoberg County. All 1,400 of them are registered and, in the vast majority of cases, something is said about their lives in North America. Only for about 10 percent is there no information at all. These losses, moreover, are mainly for the earlier generations, which have been difficult to trace for chronological reasons. Silence here does not normally mean failure. Of those who left Långasjö after the turn of the century, it can be established that almost every one found acceptable occupations and homesteads in North America. The conclusion must be that very few of these rural emigrants have totally failed or been forgotten.

A similar conclusion has been reached through a much more limited investigation of my own relatives: grand-uncles, second and third cousins, and so on. The great majority of them managed pretty well in the new country. Very few disappeared or failed totally.

In any event, there was a measure of tragedy which often struck both the emigrants and their relatives very strongly. One concrete example may be given. In 1866, two young boys left a small croft in Ryssby, Kronoberg County. Their parents and a small sister stayed at home. The brothers hoped to return and buy a farm for their parents, who were hard-pressed with work for the manor which owned their croft. The sister was promised a pair of boots, as relief from her wooden clogs. The two emigrants worked as farmhands, stonecutters, and horse custodians in Colorado. In his last letter, one of the brothers described how he sat on a horse's back and caught wild horses with a lasso. In 1889, after twenty-three years, they promised to come at Christmas. But they did not arrive at the festive Christmas table. On Christmas morning the family went to church, hoping to see the two men there. Some visitors came wearing American furs, but not the expected ones. Then the family went several times to the railway station, asking in vain for letters. After a month, they gave up, "but Mother went on waiting until her old age."

PASTORS

Of all organizations founded by Swedish Americans, the Augustana Synod — or, from 1948, the Augustana Church — has been the largest and most important. It was started in 1860, in the same year as the Augustana Seminary and College in Chicago. In 1863, it was moved to Paxton, Illinois, and in 1875 to Rock Island, Illinois. The church existed until 1962, when it was merged with the Lutheran Church of America which has now, in its turn, merged with a bigger Lutheran church.

From 1860 until 1962 at the Augustana Synod, 2,500 pastors were ordained. Before 1914, most of them had been born in

Sweden. After that, sons and grandsons of Swedish immigrants predominated. Very few of the pastors had no Swedish background at all. The total number of Swedish-born pastors was 876, a remarkable group in Swedish American history.

The Augustana Synod was deeply rooted in rural Lutheran piety and was faithful to the Church of Sweden, sometimes regarded as a "mother church". The original orientation was Low Church, which meant some scepticism about the hierarchical system in Sweden and a positive attitude toward evangelical lay activities. The Augustana pastors became ever more orthodox in their Lutheran theology, with a growing High Church orientation, but still lacking bishops.

All the leading pioneers in the Synod were natives of poor families in typical emigrant districts. The first president, Tuve Nilsson Hasselquist, was born in Osby, Kristianstad County. Lars Paul Esbjörn, the first president of the Seminary, was born at Delsbo in Hälsingland, the son of a parish tailor. He had served as a pastor in Sweden and returned there already in 1863. Erland Carlsson was born in Älghult, Kronoberg County, and had also been a pastor before emigrating, but stayed in America until his death. Jonas Swensson, the second president of the Synod, was born in Våthult, Jönköping County. Eric Norelius, the historiographer of the Synod, was a native of Hassela in Hälsingland.

Among the 876 Swedish-born pastors, the rural districts in southern Sweden were overrepresented, reflecting their old Lutheran traditions. The central and northern provinces, more influenced by evangelical, free-church movements, were underrepresented. Fairly many Augustana pastors were born in Värmland, but this province was less prominent among the Augustana pastors than in the total Swedish American stock.

A clear majority of the Swedish-born pastors, probably around 75 percent, came from the old peasant "estate" and similar rural strata. The lower middle class had some representa-

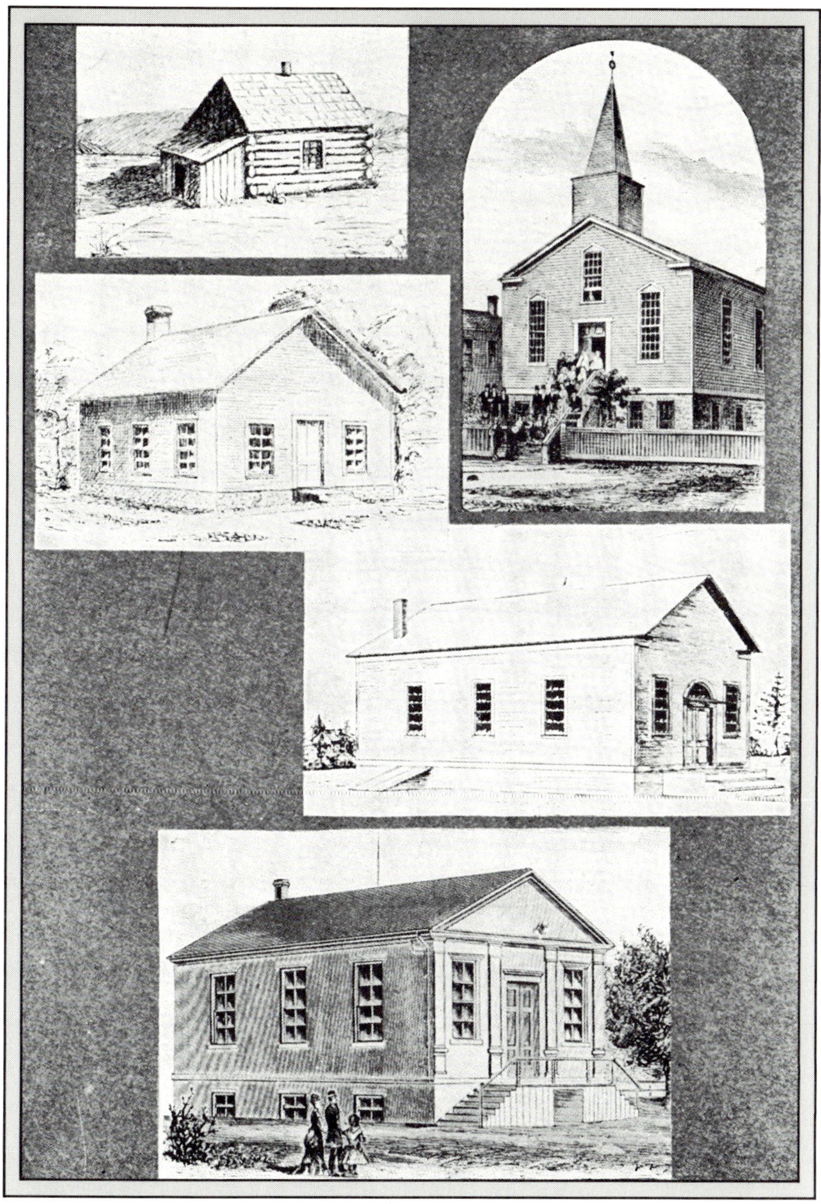

*Early Swedish Lutheran churches in Illinois. Included
are the Immanuel Church of Chicago (upper right) and
the church in Andover (below).*

tives, whereas very few of the pastors were sons of clergymen, higher civil servants, or other people of standing. Consequently, the Augustana Synod had a broader recruitment than the clergy at home, even though this group was more "popular" than any comparable professional category in Sweden.

It is symptomatic that almost 30 percent of the Augustana pastors had the typical Swedish peasant surnames: Johnson, Anderson, Nelson, Carlson, and the like. This kind of name has also been common in the Lutheran Church in America. For many poor sons of farmers and crofters, who found the ordinary Swedish education at secondary schools and universities much too long and expensive, the Augustana education opened an easier path to advancement. A minority of the Augustana pastors, around sixty, returned to Sweden some years after their ordination, in order to enter the Church of Sweden, where they were normally accepted despite their relatively low level of education. One of them, residing at Sorunda, Södermanland, in a "large and beautiful vicarage", wrote in 1937, "I am grateful to America, I am grateful to Sweden, I am grateful to God."

The Augustana Church finally embraced some half million members — a considerable part of the Swedish stock, although far from the majority. For the Swedish identity and cultural heritage in America, the church has played an enormous role. It has helped to found four colleges which still exist: Augustana College (1860), Gustavus Adolphus College at St. Peter, Minnesota (1862), Bethany College at Lindsborg, Kansas (1869), and Upsala College at East Orange, New Jersey (1893). Many leading Swedish American scholars, writers, and politicians have been educated at these colleges, where Swedish traditions and connections are preserved in spite of the inevitable Americanization. The Augustana Synod has also started a number of hospitals, children's homes, and homes for the aged.

One example of an Augustana career is provided by Petri Magni LeVander, ordained as pastor in 1907 at New Britain,

*Old Swedish cemetery at Lindstrom, Chisago County, Minnesota.
The gravestones have Swedish names, such as Ingrid Andersdotter
and John Pettersson. The town is named after an early settler,
Daniel Lindstrom, a native of Hassela, Hälsingland. At Lindstrom,
"Karl Oskar Days" are celebrated every year, after the main
character in Vilhelm Moberg's great epos.*

Connecticut. He was a native of Urshult, Kronoberg County, the son of a clergyman — N.P. Löfvander — and an unmarried girl. In America, where he arrived in 1892, the young man changed the spelling of his surname. He died in 1936 at Watertown, Minnesota. One of his sons became governor of Minnesota, and another is a prominent lawyer in Minneapolis.

Emigrants with a free-church background also founded organizations in America. The most important is the Swedish Evangelical Mission Covenant in America, formed in 1885. It is now the only religious denomination of Swedish origin in North America, although it has changed its name to the Evangelical Covenant Church of America. Its Swedish counterpart is *Svenska Missionsförbundet*, and its geographical origin seems to have been about the same as that of the mother organization — primarily Värmland, Jönköping and Örebro Counties. The first president, Carl August Björk, was a native of Lommaryd in Jönköping County; the most famous preacher, Erik August Skogsbergh, was born in Värmland. In 1894, the Covenant Church founded North Park College in Chicago, whose first president, David Nyvall, came from Karlskoga, which, though in Värmland, belongs to Örebro County. Both the church and the college have preserved a good deal of their Swedish heritage.

The Swedish Baptists and Methodists, too, once had their own churches and colleges in the United States. Bethel College in St. Paul, Minnesota, nowadays called The Bethel College and Seminary, is rooted in Swedish Baptist activities. The guiding light among Swedish American Methodists was Olof Gustaf Hedström, born at Nottebäck in Kronoberg County. As early as 1845, he formed in New York the first Swedish Methodist congregation in America. The Mormons have a Swedish element as well, but no special Swedish congregations.

A notable aspect of the Swedish religious endeavors in North America, particularly in the Augustana Church, was the transference of the Swedish churchbook registry tradition to the New World. As a result, the members of Swedish congregations have been far better recorded than Americans as a rule. But unlike their counterparts in the Church of Sweden, the Swedish American pastors were responsible only for those who had voluntarily entered their congregations.

Although Lutherans have been the largest religious group among Swedish Americans, they have never amounted to a majority. Today, the Swedish Americans belong to various denominations, and many to none at all. The Swedish language was, in principle, abandoned during the decades between the World Wars, when a growing number of the young became unable to follow Swedish sermons — yet it is still used at Christmas. Some features of Swedish piety can still be found in Swedish American homes. For example, the table prayers have sometimes been kept in the old language, even by those who do not fully understand their meaning.

THE TWO MAINSTREAMS IN
SWEDISH AMERICAN CULTURE
Newspapers and Organizations

We have seen that clear differences existed in the Swedish American industrial establishment as regards social origin and educational level. The building contractors and carpenters had a rural, agrarian background and a rather limited theoretical education. The engineers were more urban, more middle-class, and better educated. This cleft can also be observed in the cultural sector.

The Augustana pastors and congregations made up a counterpart to the contractors. Mostly from villages and farms, they were strongly Lutheran and conservative, moral and puritan, connected in America with the Republican Party, very patriotic as both Swedes and Americans. This group had many spokesmen in the numerous Swedish newspapers in North America, usually published once or twice a week, and often short-lived but, in some cases, quite vigorous.

The outstanding example was *Hemlandet*, the first regular Swedish newspaper in America, started by Hasselquist in Gales-

The initiation staff of the Independent Order of Svithiod, Chicago.
The strong female element is striking.

burg, Illinois, in 1855. It moved to Chicago in 1859, with Eric
Norelius and his cousin Jonas Engberg as editors. After some
changes, Johan Enander took over the responsibility in 1869 and
placed his stamp upon the publication for several decades. He
was born in Härja, Skaraborg County, the son of a farmer. In
1869, he emigrated to the United States and, like many other
poor immigrants with an interest in higher studies, he intended
to be an Augustana pastor. But chance soon altered his plans. As
a journalist he was very successful, leaning strongly on the Augustana conservative ideals, highly critical of secular activities
such as theatre and profane music. He combined veneration of
Swedish tradition — symbolized by monarchy, church, and de-

fense organization — with loyalty to the American presidents, as long as they belonged to the Republican Party.

Many of the leading Swedes in Chicago, however, had other ideas and ambitions. One was the businessman Charles John Sundell, born in Stockholm to an artisan. He emigrated in 1850 and reached Chicago in 1853. Four years later, he founded a Swedish association, *Svea*, whose purpose was to present "elevating and ennobling entertainment". The interest in nonreligious literature, as well as in music and theatre, became strong. The members came largely from urban middle-class families.

This group of Chicago Swedes got its own newspaper in 1866, *Svenska Amerikanaren*. Colonel Hans Mattson, the editor, was assisted by Herman Roos, who soon took over the editorship. Roos was born at Järpås, Skaraborg County, the son of an army captain from the old noble family Roos af Hjelmsäter. He had studied at Uppsala and Lund, and worked for newspapers in Stockholm, before emigrating in 1864. The fledgling newspaper declared itself as liberal and "benevolently neutral towards Christianity". In cultural matters, it strongly opposed the conservative stand taken by *Hemlandet*. It claimed to be politically neutral but actually supported the Republican Party from a less conservative viewpoint than did *Hemlandet*. The two newspapers competed intensely until 1914, when they merged under the name of *Svenska Amerikanaren*. Called *Svenska Amerikanaren-Tribunen* since 1936, it is one of the very few Swedish newspapers in America which have survived until today.

In the meantime, a number of other Swedish newspapers were launched, such as *Svenska Amerikanska Posten* in Minneapolis (1885). It was taken over in 1887 by Swan J. Turnblad, a native of Vislanda in Kronoberg County. His large residence is now the headquarters of the American Swedish Institute in Minneapolis.

Similarly, secular societies and orders were founded, often for the purpose of mutual help. Examples are the Independent

Order of Svithiod, formed in Chicago at the end of the 1880s; the Independent Orders of Vikings, started in Chicago in 1890; *Skandinaviska Brödraförbundet* (The Scandinavian Fraternity of America), formed by Swedes in Pennsylvania in 1894; the Vasa Order of America, founded in Connecticut in 1896; and *Svenska Klubben* (Swedish Club) of Seattle, formed in 1902. Added to these were many smaller, more specialized organizations – for women, socialists, singers, Good Templars, and provincial groups, such as *Norrlands Gille* and *Westgöta Gille*.

However, the religious denominations always had a larger membership than the secular ones. The churches were more flexible, for instance on the language question, and could adapt themselves better to the demands of the younger generations. In 1936–37, the Swedish American religious organizations had a total membership of 365,000, whereof the Augustana Synod alone had 255,000. The nationwide "fraternal organizations" had only 110,000, whereof the Vasa Order of America comprised 56,000. After that, secular organizations – except the Vasa Order – declined in membership or disappeared. The number of provincial clubs or *gillen* in Chicago, for example, has decreased from thirty-three in 1933 to four in 1980.

The old rivalry between the two main groups of Swedish Americans, the conservative Lutheran and the secular-liberal, no longer exists. Both have been affected by general Americanization, and the Lutherans also by secularization. Yet paradoxically, the typical Swedish heritage has its strongest remnants in its religious connections.

SCIENTISTS

Among the very early Swedish immigrants in North America, the middle class was prominent in relative terms, though not in absolute numbers. Fairly many journalists, officers, and university students emigrated before the period of mass emigration. But this category, except the engineers, was poorly represented after 1850. Very few emigrants then had Swedish university degrees, and very few went to American universities. A small minority enrolled at colleges such as Augustana, Gustavus Adolphus, and North Park — but very few prepared themselves for scientific careers.

One of the latter was Anton Julius Carlson, born on a farm in Bohuslän. In 1891, he joined an older brother in Chicago, who had sent him money for the ticket. After some time as an apprentice carpenter, he entered Augustana College and the Theological Seminary in Rock Island, aiming to become a pastor. However, the science teacher at Augustana, Johan August Udden — a native of Lekåsa in Skaraborg County, living since early childhood in America — made him change his mind. Udden himself was later a noted geologist in the Texas oil fields. Carlson became a physiologist and a famous professor at the University of Chicago. He was one of the world's leading authorities in the physiology of hunger and made important discoveries about the causes of diabetes.

In the second generation, the situation was different. Many sons and daughters of the immigrants went to colleges and universities, shaping extraordinary careers in some cases. Two Swedish Americans of the second generation have become Nobel Prize winners. In 1936, Carl David Anderson, only thirty-one years old, became co-winner of the prize in physics, for the discovery of the subatomic particles called positrons. He was born in New York City of parents from Östergötland.

The other, Glenn T. Seaborg, was awarded the prize in chemistry in 1951, together with one of his colleagues at the University of California in Berkeley, for their work on the transuranium elements such as plutonium. Seaborg was born in Michigan but came as a boy with his parents to California. His father was born in Michigan to Swedish immigrants, and his

Nobel prizewinner Dr. Glenn Seaborg and his son David visiting the Örebro County Emigrant Registrar Society, 1985, to trace their ancestry.

mother in Sweden. Moreover, his father was a master machinist – like many of Seaborg's Swedish ancestors in Värmland, Närke, and southern Dalarna. Seaborg represents the technological tradition among Swedish Americans. He is strongly aware of his Swedish background and has close contacts with the old country.

Within the humanities, historians have been notably active. Amandus Johnson, already mentioned, became the historiographer of New Sweden. The first Swedish American to make deep studies of the mass emigration was George M. Stephenson at the University of Minnesota. His grandfather came from Kalmar County to New Sweden, Iowa, as early as 1849. The Swedish Historical Society of America was founded in 1905 but faded away in the 1930s. The Swedish Pioneer Historical Society, started in Chicago in 1948, has been more successful: now called the American-Swedish Historical Society, it publishes a quarterly journal. Another such publication, the *Swedish American Genealogist*, was initiated in 1981 by Nils William Olsson, born in America of Swedish immigrants but educated partly in Sweden.

Among scholars dealing with the history of literature, Alrik Gustafson may be noticed. Born in Iowa of Swedish immigrants, he became a professor at the University of Minnesota, writing *A History of Swedish Literature* (1961) and other books.

One of the most remarkable Swedish American philologists was Hjalmar Edgren. He was born in Värmland, the son of an ironworks manager (*bruksförvaltare*), and died at Djursholm outside Stockholm. Four times during his lifetime he emigrated to the United States and returned, a rather unique record. While first in America in the 1860s, he took part in the Civil War; his last stay, in the 1890s, included a professorship at the University of Nebraska.

On the whole, Swedish American scientists and scholars have played a distinguished role in North America. Yet in spite of outstanding exceptions, their achievements cannot be compared with those of, for instance, the engineers and building contractors.

WRITERS, PAINTERS, AND COMPOSERS

Although the Swedish immigrants to America could read and, in most cases, write, their literary baggage was quite limited. They were familiar with the Bible and the Swedish *psalmbok* and therefore knew some religious poems by Wallin and Franzén. Some of them may also have read Tegnér, Runeberg, and Rydberg. But very few had studied Almqvist or, later on, Strindberg. It happened that immigrants wrote small idyllic poems in Swedish. They were, however, unable to produce qualified novels or poetry in English.

Certain Swedish authors visited North America during the period of mass emigration. Rosalie Roos, whose subsequent married name was Olivecrona, came to South Carolina in 1851 to teach music and French. She herself was no prominent writer, but she made some Americans in the South acquainted with Swedish culture. Fredrika Bremer travelled in the United States in 1849 – 51. In Iowa, one community is named Fredericka, and another Bremer. In Minnesota, still only a territory, not a state, Miss Bremer had a prophetic vision of the opportunities awaiting Swedish immigrants: "a new Scandinavia shall one day bloom in the valley of the Mississippi." Her novel *Homes of the New World* (1853 – 54) was immediately translated into English and became a success on both sides of the Atlantic. Her American experience influenced her activities in the women's movement in Sweden.

Carl Jonas Love Almqvist's stay in the United States from 1851 to 1865 had a different scenario. He escaped from justice, accused of forgery and attempted murder. In Philadelphia, he became a bigamist. His life there was miserable, but he managed to catch the emigrant's nostalgia in the words: "just Sweden Swedish gooseberries has".

Per Hallström, a young engineer and a future famous writer, lived in the United States from 1888 to 1890 – first in St. Paul, next in Newark, New Jersey, as a draughtsman, and finally in Philadelphia as a chemist at a factory. He met many German immigrants and spoke more German than English. He disliked the country for its imperialism, hypocrisy, cynicism, and materialism. Later, he continued to criticize America from a socialist, then a conservative and pro-German, standpoint.

Another Swedish writer, Henning Berger, resided in New York City (1889 – 90) and Chicago (1892 – 99). He endured numerous hardships and was sometimes unemployed. In Chicago he worked mostly as a poor clerk at the White Star Line. His attitude to the United States was ambivalent: while fascinated with the roaring metropolitan life, he was often disappointed. The immigrants in his novels are commonly rootless, but if they return to Sweden, they cannot adapt there either.

Gradually a cadre of Swedish American writers emerged, usually employing the old language. They did not reach the literary levels of, for instance, Bremer and Hallström, or of the Norwegian American author Ole Rolvaag, but their contributions are not negligible. An example was Ernst Skarstedt, the son of a Lutheran minister who became a university professor. He reached America in 1879 and became a leader among Swedish American authors and journalists. Skarstedt wrote almost entirely in Swedish and was rather critical of his home country.

Another prominent author and journalist was Vilhelm Berger, born in Värmland to an ironworks proprietor. He came to Chicago in 1896, and was especially skillful as a creator of short stories. One of them is entitled *Glad och hungrig: Minnen från mitt hundår i Amerika* (Jolly and Hungry: Memoirs of My "Dog's Year" in America). His tales are very bitter about both Sweden and America, but also highly appreciative of the Augustana Synod, Lutheran piety, and industriousness, as well as of American freedom.

The most popular Swedish American author of the first generation was Leonard Strömberg. He was born at Arboga, Västmanland County, the son of a blacksmith. Arriving in Nebraska in 1895, he went on to become Methodist minister at Oakland, California. During the 1920s and 1930s, he was one of the writers in most demand at Swedish libraries. Many of his numerous novels, printed chiefly in Sweden, are set in Swedish American environments and are shaped as a homage to Swedish honesty, piety, temperance, and endeavor. The hero may, for instance, be a poor boy who finds fortune when he saves a wealthy person's life or receives an unexpected legacy, culminating in marriage to a pleasant and well-situated girl. Strömberg personified the three features which Gustav Sundbärg — the pioneer in Swedish emigration research — has pointed out as characteristic of contemporary Swedish history: emigration, social mobility, and free-church teetotalism.

A different breed of writer was Arthur Landfors, native to Överluleå in Norrbotten County, who reached Massachusetts in 1908. Like a lot of other immigrants from northern Sweden, he belonged to the "left wing", which was often neglected by the Swedish American establishment. His poems, written in Swedish, depict the immigrant's incurable rootlessness.

In the second generation, writers of Swedish descent have normally used the English language. One of them has won a real reputation — Carl Sandburg. He was born in 1878 at Galesburg, Illinois, a town with many Swedes. His father was a blacksmith, both parents coming from Östergötland. His first vocabulary was Swedish, and his mother liked to call him to the dining-table with a Swedish phrase. He changed very early to English, however, and had difficulty in following his parents' conversation in Swedish.

Like many other children of poor immigrants, Sandburg was somewhat ashamed of his simple and foreign background, and tried to be a true American. In his poems, often dealing with Chicago, there happen to be a few Swedish surnames such as Lindquist, but no allusions to Sweden or Swedish immigration. Yet he gradually became more interested in his ancestry, and visited Sweden twice: in 1918 – 19 and 1959. During the second visit, he was informed about his parents' homes. Two Swedes captured his imagination, King Charles XII and the author Albert Engström. His great biographical work, though, was devoted to Abraham Lincoln. In any case, he has now become a symbol of the Swedish heritage in America.

Sandburg stands rather alone as a representative of Swedish

*Carl Sandburg and the Swedish Ambassador Erik Boheman in
Chicago on Sandburg's seventy-fifth birthday, 1953. Sandburg
lived then in North Carolina, on Connemara Farm, where
the main goat barn was called the Swedish House.*

America in modern American literature on the highest level.
Among writers of the second rank, the novelist Nelson Algren
may be mentioned. He was born in Detroit in 1909 and had a
Swedish grandfather. Algren drifted around the country, often
in railway boxcars, and has written about social misery and hard
times. A close friend of his was the French author Simone de
Beauvoir.

Actually, the best fictional descriptions of Swedish American life have been written in Sweden. Albin Widén, who spent
some years in the United States, created some of the first examples. Later, he was overshadowed by Vilhelm Moberg.

*Birger Sandzén at a painting easel. He liked
the mountains in Kansas.*

Swedish American painters have very seldom gained fame, apart from Hesselius — father and son — and Wertmüller. Anders Zorn spent many years in the United States and, like Wertmüller, made spectacular portraits, but he cannot be regarded as an emigrant. The most successful Swedish American painter has been Birger Sandzén, born at Blidsberg in Älvsborg County. In 1894, he came to Bethany College in Kansas. His paintings often caught the prairie landscape and the colorful mountains of the Midwest. Claes Oldenburg, born in Stockholm in 1929, but living in the United States since childhood, belongs to a younger generation. He has sometimes been called "the Picasso of Pop". Another famous painter, James A. Rosenquist, born in North Dakota in 1933, has Swedish ancestry.

Of Swedish American sculptors in America, none has been

as renowned as Carl Milles, who spent much time in America. His works are seen at many public places. He has no counterpart among the real immigrants or their descendants.

The best-known Swedish American composer is Howard Hanson, born on a farm in Nebraska in 1896, his parents coming from Lund. He is occasionally termed "the American Sibelius". The Swedish heritage, especially folk songs, played an obvious role in his music.

It can be concluded that Swedish Americans have made their mark in American literature, art, and music; some of their achievements are outstanding. Still, it is impossible to count these contributions among the most typical Swedish elements in American life. In only one field have Swedes held leading positions in American culture — the scenic arts.

ACTRESSES AND ACTORS

In 1850, Jenny Lind, the "Swedish nightingale", arrived in New York. Her thirty-seven public appearances there were met with enthusiasm. During the next two years, she visited several other American cities, and people spoke of "Jenny Lind fever", "Jenny rage", or "Lindomania". One of her admirers, the poet Henry Wadsworth Longfellow, said that she sang "like the morning star; clear, liquid, heavenly sounds".

Jenny Lind was followed in 1870 by Christina Nilsson, born in Vederslöv, Kronoberg County, the daughter of a crofter. The American critics found in her song the same combination of strength and sweetness as in Jenny Lind's performances. In two years, she gave no less than 261 concerts in fifty-four cities. She visited the country again in the 1870s and 1880s.

These two great female artists have been the precursors of a series of successful Swedish actresses and singers coming to the United States in our century. Some of them — such as Karin

Branzell, Kerstin Thorborg, Ingrid Bergman, Göta Ljungberg, and Birgit Nilsson — have spent much time in America without being rooted there. Others have found a permanent residence, most conspicuously Greta Garbo, born in Stockholm in 1905 and living in the United States since 1925. No Swedish immi-

*Greta Garbo as Queen Christina, in the film of the same name
(1934), the eighteenth of the twenty-four films she made in the
United States. The film was criticized in Sweden because of
its almost total lack of historical authenticity. It may be added that
Greta Garbo was much more beautiful than the queen.*

grant has won such renown as this enigmatic, "divine" actress, whose Nordic beauty has been able to portray Queen Christina as well as Ninotchka and Anna Karenina.

Also settled in America more or less for life have been Signe Hasso, Viveca Lindfors, and Ann-Margret Olson. A whole career in America was made by Anna Q. Nilsson, born at Ystad in Skåne. Susan Hayward, born in Brooklyn, had a Swedish background. Gloria Swanson was born in Chicago to an army captain, a son of Swedish immigrants. Myrna Loy had a Swedish grandmother. Inga Swenson, active in the 1980s, has Swedish ancestry.

Compared with this brilliant female roster, its male counterparts seem less impressive, although far from dull. Jussi Björling, Set Svanholm, and Einar Ekberg have had great success as guest singers in the United States. Warner Oland, a native of Västerbotten County, became famous in his role as the Chinese detective, Charlie Chan. Edgar Bergen, born in Chicago in 1903 of immigrants from Hässleholm, Kristianstad County, is said to have elevated ventriloquism from a vaudeville act to a fine art. Richard Widmark, born in Minnesota of Swedish ancestry, has represented old Viking ideals in Wild Western guise.

The most striking achievements by male Swedish artists in North America are to be found in stage management. The two great pioneers of Swedish film history, Mauritz Stiller and Victor Sjöström, gained inspiration as film producers during their visits to the United States. In recent times, Alf Kjellin has been a successful producer in American television.

POLITICIANS

When a poor immigrant settles in a foreign country to start a new life, he has much more to think about at first than his role on the political scene. The pressing problems of assimilation and the daily struggle for survival claim most of his powers. Moreover, even in the United States, which has shown great generosity toward strangers, legislation sets certain formal restrictions on the newcomer. A period of residence in the country, and in each state, has normally been required before a person is eligible to vote.

The Swedes who came to the United States in the 1850s and 1860s took little part in politics. But the Civil War led them into some political and military activity. Around 3,000 Swedes fought for the Unionist cause, very few being enrolled in the Confederate states' army.

From then on, the overwhelming majority of the Swedes were Republicans, although almost none earned any political post. In Illinois, this situation lasted until 1874, before the first Swedes gained seats in the state legislature. Their numbers were high in the state, yet amounted to only 3 percent of its population.

In Minnesota, however, the Swedes soon made up nearly 15 percent of the inhabitants, and the total Scandinavian share was about 30 percent. The leading Republicans, most of them Yankees who had migrated from New York or New England, looked down on Scandinavians as "voting cattle" who could always be relied upon for support, whether or not the party did anything for them as an ethnic group. But in the 1880s, the local Democrats – largely Germans and Irishmen – discovered that they could win marginal voters by introducing Scandinavian, mostly Norwegian, candidates. So the Republicans were gradually forced to react with their own Scandinavian candidates.

In this way the Norwegians, and next the Swedes, began to enter leading posts in Minnesota. The first Swede in the state legislature had been elected in 1865. In 1870, Colonel Hans Mattson, known for his service in the Civil War, became Secretary of State. A more important step was taken in 1886, when the Republican John Lind — born at Kånna in Kronoberg County — was elected to the U.S. House of Representatives for a district in southern Minnesota. He was reelected in 1888 and 1890, and became governor of the state in 1898. By then, he had changed his political stance because of the Republican policy on gold. He belonged to the "Silver Republicans", who cooperated with the Democrats. Had he not been supported by a lot of Scandinavian marginal voters, especially Swedish, he would not have been elected in this otherwise strongly Republican state.

Lind was defeated, though, when he ran for reelection in 1900. Opposed to him were some Augustana voters, who complained that he had abandoned the Lutheran faith and joined the Methodists. But in 1904 a Democrat, John Albert Johnson — born in St. Peter, Minnesota, of poor parents, the father from Jönköping County and the mother from Östergötland — was elected governor, the rest of the state administration staying in Republican hands. As in 1898, the effect of the Scandinavian marginal voters was decisive.

Johnson was regarded as a prototype of the American self-made man. He was a strong and popular governor, reelected in 1906 and 1908. Finally, he was mentioned as a possible Presidential candidate and, had he not died in 1909, might well have been chosen to head the Democratic party ticket in the 1912 national elections — instead of Woodrow Wilson. His statue stands today outside the State Capitol in St. Paul, together with that of the Norwegian-born governor and U.S. senator, Knute Nelson.

The Scandinavians were now a dominant group in Minnesota politics. From 1892 — when Knute Nelson became governor — until 1983, all but four of the state's governors had a Scandinavian background. It was said in the 1930s that Minnesota did not care about the governor's origins, as long as he was a Scandinavian. Many of the U.S. senators and congressmen from Minnesota, and members of the state legislature, have also been Scandinavian.

Compared with the Germans, the Scandinavians have been clearly overrepresented. This must be due to the religious division among the Germans, and to their lack of a common constitutional and national tradition; in 1914, political difficulties made their position still more complicated. The Norwegians and Swedes usually cooperated with ease, even during the Union conflicts in Scandinavia until 1905. On the local level, the Norwegians were better represented than the Swedes, because of the denser Norwegian settlement in rural areas, especially in western Minnesota. The Swedish population outside the Chisago-Kanabec-Isanti area was more urban and more scattered.

Some Swedes outside Minnesota, too, won prominent political positions. A rather odd figure was Frederick Lundin, who had come from Östergötland to Chicago with his parents in the 1880s. After some years as a newspaper-boy, boot-cleaner, and shop-salesman, he and a brother started, in 1889, a firm selling a much-appreciated juniper beer. He joined the Republican Party and, in 1910 – 11, belonged to the U.S. House of Representatives, the first Swede representing Illinois there. Later, he remained strong in Chicago politics, partly thanks to underworld connections.

World War I created a number of problems for Swedes in America. Traditionally, many of them felt strong ties with Germany, especially with its Lutherans. But after America entered the war in 1917, most Swedish Americans loyally sided with the Wilson administration. In the House of Representatives, the declaration of war was supported by three congressmen of Swedish ancestry, all born in America: Irvine Lenroot of Wisconsin, whose parents came from Skåne and Värmland; Sidney Anderson of Minnesota, who also had Norwegian parentage;

and Charles O. Lobeck of Nebraska, with partly German parentage. In spite of this vote, Lenroot — a member of the progressive, less capitalistic wing of the Republican party — was severely criticized by President Wilson during the senatorial elections of 1918. Though loyal to the American cause, he was accused of seeking support from traitors, pro-German sympathizers, rebels, and pacifists. Lenroot won the election anyway, becoming the first Swedish American in the U.S. senate. In 1920, he was mentioned as a possible vice-presidential candidate.

Lenroot's position on the war issue was shared by ex-Governor John Lind, then the special Presidential Emissary to Mexico, and by J. A. A. Burnquist, governor of Minnesota, born in Iowa of Swedish parentage. Despite his ethnic origin, Burnquist went to such lengths in his patriotic fervor that he advocated a ban on foreign-language instruction in American schools. He felt that all immigrants should either adopt the English language or risk deportation.

There was, however, some Swedish American opposition to President Wilson's foreign policy. The most outspoken isolationist was Charles A. Lindbergh, born in Stockholm in 1858 but taken by his parents to Minnesota a year later. His father, Ola Månsson, mentioned earlier, had belonged to the Swedish Estate of Peasants. Lindbergh became a lawyer in Minnesota and was elected in 1906 to the U.S. House of Representatives, joining the progressive wing of the Republican party. To some extent he represented the Populist tradition in the Midwest, opposing big business, trust and railway companies, while appealing to rural and small-town votes rather than big-city constituencies.

Lindbergh, during the House session of 1916, spoke clearly against any American intervention in the war. The same year he tried to reach the Senate but was defeated. After America entered the war, he wrote a book criticizing official U.S. foreign policy. In 1918, he ran for governor of Minnesota against Burnquist, but lost by a narrow margin in the Republican primary elections. Though bitterly accused of deficient loyalty and patriotism, he received many votes, especially from Scandinavian and German voters.

In 1917, fifty members of the House of Representatives voted against the declaration of war. Two of them were of Norwegian descent, and one had a Swedish background – Ernest Lundeen, a Minnesota Republican, born in South Dakota of Swedish parents. Lundeen felt that he had the support of broad popular opinion, particularly among Swedish Americans. According to him, both Great Britain and Germany had violated American shipping rights, and he considered the Scandinavian countries' policy of neutrality to be worthy of imitation. Ex-President Theodore Roosevelt called him "a shadow Hun", but later admitted that his loyalty could not be questioned, even though he was wrong. Lundeen lost a bid for reelection in 1918. He returned to the House in 1933, still an isolationist, yet at the same time a warm supporter of Franklin Roosevelt's New Deal. Finally, in 1937 – 40, he was a member of the U.S. Senate.

After World War I, fairly many Scandinavians in Minnesota joined the Farmer Labor party there, voicing the unrest which had seized farmers and workers. Lindbergh, one of the party's leading candidates, ran for the House of Representatives and then for the U.S. Senate, but lost to other Scandinavians. More successful was Magnus Johnson, born in Värmland, where he had worked as a glass-blower and been influenced by early Swedish socialist activities. Johnson emigrated to America in 1891 and became a farmer in Minnesota, joining the farmers' cooperative movement. In 1923 as a Farmer Labor candidate he was elected to the U.S. Senate – a great surprise and annoyance to aristocratic senators. During his short term, he attracted much attention with his Swedish Värmland accent, demands for socialization, extreme opinions on farming, and call for Amer-

*Campaign poster for Charles A. Lindbergh during his first
Congressional campaign, 1906. He was elected by the 6th District in
Minnesota, where the German element was strong, but where the
Swedes were also numerous. Many German and Swedish farmers and
laborers supported Lindbergh's progressive, anticapitalist, and
isolationist ideas. Many followed him when he left the Republican
Party and joined first the Non-Partisan League and then the Farmer
Labor Party. His son, Charles A. Lindbergh, Jr., joined
his father's unsuccessful campaign in 1923, when his father
experienced his first airplane ride. Lindbergh Sr. died in 1924.*

ican recognition of the Soviet Union. He failed in his 1924 bid
for reelection, but in 1932 he won a seat in the House, strongly
supported by the voters. Of nine Minnesota congressmen then
elected, six were Scandinavians. Despite his popularity, Johnson
lost in 1934.

The Farmer Labor party remained a vital factor in Minnesota political life. Floyd Björnstjerne Olson became especially famous. He was born in Minneapolis of poor parents, a father from Tröndelagen in Norway and a mother from Värmland. From 1931 until his death in 1936, he served as governor and was sometimes thought a strong, radical rival to Franklin Roosevelt for the presidency. Yet Olson himself supported Roosevelt and the New Deal. By American standards, he was very radical indeed – although hardly a Communist, as some antagonists claimed. He favored the workers in general strikes, but avoided extremes. He strove for the introduction of unemployment compensation benefits and general pension programs, as well as interest and mortgage allowances for indebted farmers.

In many ways, Olson resembled his Swedish contemporary, Per Albin Hansson, leader of the Social Democratic Party, who also emphasized solidarity between farmers and workers. Like Hansson, Olson had more sympathy with the workers than with farmers, and among the latter he apparently lost votes towards the end of his career. Probably Olson was influenced by Swedish politics on certain issues. He occasionally used the slogan "the Swedish middle way", as did the American writer Marquis W. Childs in his well-known book *Sweden: The Middle Way* (1936). It is sometimes said that the rather advanced social legislation in Minnesota is due to the strong Scandinavian influence.

At all events, it is strange that so many of the leading Swedish American politicians of this period – Charles Lindbergh, Magnus Johnson, Floyd Olson and others – had clear radical tendencies. They cannot, of course, be called representative of most Swedish Americans. The latter were generally conservative, while not as ultraconservative as many Swedes have imagined them to be. An example was Carl R. Chindblom of Chicago, born there of parents from Östergötland, and a U.S. congressman from 1919 to 1933. Yet the radical politicians had support within their own ethnic group, and some Swedish Americans were far more radical than any member of congress.

A prototype here was the celebrated Joe Hill, originally named Joel Hägglund. In 1902, he left his native town Gävle for the United States, where he joined the syndicalist organization Industrial Workers of the World. His political activity led to a tragic end. In 1915, he was executed in Salt Lake City, Utah, condemned for murder on the basis of vague evidence, despite his own denial and Swedish diplomatic protests. His revolutionary songs are still alive.

Joe Hill represented only a small minority of Swedish Americans. There were, however, some socialist tendencies on the local level in Swedish American communities dominated by industrial workers. Mayor Samuel A. Carlson of Jamestown, New York, whose parents came from Jönköping County and who was the leading politician in his city from 1908 to 1938, was sometimes regarded as a socialist, because he fought for a city-owned electric-power plant. Similar attitudes existed among the Swedish Americans in Rockford, Illinois. It should be added that some Swedish socialists emigrated for political reasons, after conflicts on the labor market — for instance from Ljusne, Hälsingland, in 1906. Many Swedes were active in the American labor movement and sometimes had their own trade unions. Lawrence P. Lindelof, born in Malmö, was president of the International Brotherhood of Painters and Allied Trades, with over 200,000 members, between the years 1929 and 1952.

Since World War II, some Swedish Americans have played important roles in both of the large American parties. An influential Democrat, Warren Magnuson of Washington State, born in Minnesota, was a U.S. congressman (1937 — 44) and senator (1944 — 81). Another well-known Democrat of Swedish descent was Clinton P. Anderson, whose father was born at Svärdsjö in Dalarna. He was U.S. Secretary of Agriculture in 1945 — 48 and after that served as a senator for New Mexico. A third Democrat of Swedish descent (third generation), Orville L. Freeman, served as governor of Minnesota (1955 – 61) and U.S. Secretary of Agriculture (1961 – 69). Most famous in the Republican party has been John B. Anderson of Rockford, born there in a Swedish family, the father having come from Älvsborg County. In the mid-1970s, he was chairman of the Republican Conference in the U.S. House of Representatives. At the same time, the corresponding chairman in the Senate was Carl T. Curtis of Nebraska, whose grandfather came from Östergötland. However, Anderson has left his party to take a radical stance. In the Presidential elections of 1980, he campaigned as an independent, appealing mainly to the young progressive voters. He received 5.5 million votes, 7 percent of the electorate – a high share for an independent candidate.

Yet the total number of Swedish American members of the U.S. Congress has been rather limited: at least thirteen in the Senate and around fifty in the House of Representatives. Swedish Americans have been more successful on the state level. At least twenty-eight have been governors: ten in Minnesota, three in Montana, three in Nebraska, two in Colorado, and ten in other states.

Illinois has had a governor of Swedish descent since 1977. James R. Thompson, a leading man in the Republican party, was born in Chicago – his mother being from Varberg in Halland – and studied at North Park College. In Minnesota, the present Lieutenant Governor, Marlene Johnson, has a Swedish background and is among the few Swedish American women making a political career. Also in Minnesota, the Secretary of State, Joan Anderson Growe, has Swedish ancestry. The present governor of Nebraska, Kay Orr, née Stark, is a third female politician of Swedish descent; she was born in Iowa. Among the governors of Montana, J. Hugo Aronson was born at Gällstad in Älvsborg County. He reached Montana in 1914, where a brakeman put him off a freight train, and in 1953 he was elected

*Future Chief Justice Earl Warren, who, as Governor of California,
received the Great Cross of the Nordstjärna Order
from the Swedish government.*

governor. The old Swedish state, Delaware, has relatively few
Swedes nowadays, but between 1969 and 1972, there was a
governor of Swedish parentage: Russel W. Peterson, born in
Wisconsin of parents from Jönköping County.

The most renowned governor of Swedish descent has been
Earl Warren, born in Los Angeles of a Norwegian father and a
Swedish mother from Hälsingland. He himself married a native
of Gotland. Besides serving as governor of California (1943 –
53) and chief justice of the U.S. Supreme Court (1953 – 69), he
was a candidate for Vice President in 1948. He belonged to the
liberal wing of the Supreme Court, taking a humanitarian stance
towards, for example, the Indian minority. Warren was suc-

ceeded as chief justice by Warren E. Burger, whose wife has a Swedish background, and he was, in his turn, followed by the present chief justice, William H. Rehnquist, whose grandfather came from Östergötland; he belongs to the conservative part of the Court.

Swedish American politicians have represented all sectors of the political spectrum, from ultraconservative to ultraradical, but perhaps somewhat concentrated in the centre. For some of them, like Charles Lindbergh and Magnus Johnson, old Swedish traditions of local self-government may have played a role.

The ethnic background of these politicians had obvious importance for their careers around the turn of the century, at least in Minnesota. Yet today this factor is quite marginal. Nor are they known to have taken any prominent part in the political relations between the United States and Sweden. President Eisenhower, whose mother-in-law's family came from Halland, said some critical words about Sweden in 1960 in Chicago, although without naming the country — he mentioned, for instance, the high rate of suicide. But during a visit to Sweden two years later, he apologized for his remarks, which were based on an article in an unreliable American magazine.

Relations with Sweden became more complicated for President Nixon. After a statement about the Vietnam War by Prime Minister Olof Palme, the President sent a protest in 1972 to the Swedish Embassy in Washington. The bearer of this unpleasant message was a Swedish American, the Under Secretary of State, U. Alexis Johnson, formerly Ambassador to Japan. Johnson, born at Falun, Kansas, is one of the rather few distinguished American diplomats of Swedish descent. Another is Franklin Forsberg, U.S. Ambassador to Sweden in 1981 – 85, born in Salt Lake City of a father from Dalarna and a mother from Gotland. The present U.S. ambassador to Sweden, Gregory J. Newell, has some Swedish ancestry, too.

During the 1980s, there have been no serious problems in

During the celebrations of the 300th anniversary of the foundation of the New Sweden colony, Crown Prince Gustaf Adolf of Sweden was unable to make a speech due to illness. His son, 26-year-old Prince Bertil, had to stand in, and his reading of his father's speech, in the pattering rain, was much appreciated. President Roosevelt (to the left in the picture) mentioned in his reply that two of his ancestors had Swedish backgrounds. The ceremony took place on June 27, 1938, in Wilmington, Delaware.

American-Swedish political relations. In the United States, the general attitude toward Sweden is friendly among the public as well as among Swedish American politicians and public officials.

CONCLUSIONS

The Swedish Americans — using this term in a wide sense — have never included more than 2 percent of the people in the United States. We cannot expect to meet members of this small minority very often in different areas of American history. In some fields, their contributions have been quite limited. However, in others they have succeeded out of proportion to their numbers. At the top of American society, Swedes and their descendants have made remarkable contributions as engineers, shipbuilders, air pioneers, building contractors, actresses, and state governors. On a broader base, such categories as pastors, farmers, lumberjacks, metalworkers, carpenters, tailors, seamstresses, and maidservants deserve recognition.

Inevitably, their Swedishness has become weaker from decade to decade in both language and culture. Especially difficult, at least for the Swedish language, was the period from World War I until the end of the 1920s. After that, changes have been more gradual. The Swedes have become Americanized more rapidly than many other groups, not due to psychological factors, but as a result of high literacy, the similarity between Swedish and English, the Protestant tradition, and the Swedes' geographical diffusion as well as concentration in urban districts. There has been no basic difference between Swedes and, for instance, the Norwegians and Germans — who have, however, been more concentrated in rural areas.

The changes in attitudes are harder to detect than the linguistic transition. Evidently Swedes of the second generation often had the same feeling as many other immigrant groups: they were somewhat ashamed of their foreign origins and longed to be transformed into true Americans as soon as possible. The third generation, growing up in an irreproachably American environment, has found it easier to regard foreign ancestry as something special and attractive — a "feather in the hat" which should be noticed and studied. Nonetheless, many Swedish Americans of the third and fourth generations care little about their background and do not identify themselves with the old country in any relevant way. Further, most of them have a mixed ancestry, and sometimes they prefer other connections than the Swedish ones.

Consequently, many Swedish American organizations have ceased to operate. But some cultural and historical associations have survived. In 1973 three of these — the Swedish Pioneer Historical Society, the American Swedish Historical Foundation in Philadelphia, and the American Swedish Institute in Minneapolis — created a coordinating body called the Swedish Council of America. Since then, other Swedish associations have joined this council, which combines the traditions of the seventeenth century with those of the mass emigration.

The Swedish heritage is fighting a hard struggle against time. Yet one element endures without any real difficulty: the family names. The vast majority of immigrants kept their old Swedish last names, either unchanged — at least in spelling, as with Anderson, Carlson, Olson, Berglund, Lindberg, and Nyberg — or with a slight change, as in Johnson, Nelson, Swanson, Nystrom, and more obviously in Sandburg, Seashore, and Youngdale. Any extensive list of American names, as in a telephone book, film credit, or editorial enumeration, normally displays some Scandinavian or even Swedish names.

In addition, some factors are hampering the widespread and inevitable Americanization. Education is increasing in both countries and, above all, improved transatlantic travel enables second and third cousins to visit each other. The developing pluralism in American society has also played a role. It is no longer so natural to regard America as a melting-pot where people from all over the world — whites, blacks, Orientals, Christians, Jews, Moslems — are eventually recast as Americans. The melting-pot view may, to be sure, have regained some ground in the patriotic 1980s. But it is still quite acceptable to emphasize one's own roots, be they Scandinavian, African, Mexican, Italian, or Irish. The Swedes have not been notably eager in their search for historical identity, yet they have taken part in the process.

Among the immigrants, it was sometimes said that Sweden was their dear old mother, and America their beloved bride. Now "mother Svea" has been replaced by a grandmother or great-grandmother, telling quaint tales for their grandchildren and singing — in a feeble voice — the old national songs. This Swedish American culture is much more than a curiosity. It is, among other things, the expression of a transatlantic sense of community, whose continuing existence is a prerequisite for the survival of Western civilization.

REFERENCES

As a rule, only works that have been used directly for the respective chapters
are listed here. Further bibliographies are in:

O.F. Ander, *The Cultural Heritage of the Swedish Immigrant*, Augustana
Library Publication 27. Rock Island, Illinois, 1956.

H. Runblom & H. Norman (eds.), "From Sweden to America", *Studia Historica Upsaliensia* 74. Minneapolis and Uppsala, 1976.

INTRODUCTION

A. Johnson, *The Swedish Settlements on the Delaware: their History and Relation to
the Indians, Dutch and English, 1638–1664*, Vols. 1–2. University of Pennsylvania 1911.

Runblom & Norman 1976.

Twentieth Census of the United States: Population. 1980

THE SWEDISH AND FINNISH COLONISTS ON THE DELAWARE

N. Ahnlund, *Nya Sverige*. Stockholm 1938.

S. Bergh (ed.), *Svenska riksrådets protokoll* 8–15 (1640–53). Stockholm 1898–1920.

Handel och Sjöfart, Vol. 196. Riksarkivet, Stockholm.

Handlingar rörande Skandinaviens historia 29. Stockholm 1848.

R.W. Harper, "När Sverige skulle bli en världsmakt", in Lindberg 1986.

T. Campanius Holm, *Kort beskrifning om provincien Nya Swerige uti America*.
Stockholm 1702.

Johnson 1911.

P. Kalm, *En resa till Norra Amerika*, Tilläggsband (ed. F. Elfving). Skrifter utg.
av Svenska Litteratursällskapet i Finland, 210. Helsingfors 1929.

R. Kero, "Värmlandsfinnar i Nya Sverige", *Värmlandsfinnar* (ed. S.
Huovinen). Stockholm 1986.

A.C. Leiby, *The Early Dutch and Swedish Settlers of New Jersey*. Princeton,
New Jersey, 1964.

G. Lindberg (ed.), *Det började i Delaware*. Stockholm 1986.

H. Linderholm, *Nya Sveriges historia*. Stockholm 1976.

E.A. Louhi, *The Delaware Finns, Or the First Permanent Settlements in Pennsylvania, Delaware, West New Jersey and Eastern Part of Maryland*. New York 1925.

F. Nordström, "Olof Stille of New Sweden", in *Swedish American Genealogist* 1986.

R.K. Turp, *West Jersey Under Four Flags*. Philadelphia 1975.

THE DESCENDANTS OF THE COLONISTS OF NEW SWEDEN

A. Benson & N. Hedin (eds.), *Swedes in America 1638–1938*. New York 1938.

S. Carlsson, "John Hanson's Swedish background", *The Swedish Pioneer Historical Quarterly*, 1978.

Church registers (New Sweden area), Uppsala domkapitels arkiv, Vol. F:VIII:6,8. Landsarkivet, Uppsala.

P.S. Craig & R. H. Hulan, *Memberships of Swedish Lutheran Churches at Racoon and Penns Neck, New Jersey (1771)*. Unpublished.

P.S. Craig & H.W. Yocom, "The Yocums of Aronameck in Philadelphia, 1648–1702", *National Genealogical Society Quarterly* 71, 1983.

Handel och Sjöfart, Vol. 196. Riksarkivet, Stockholm.

G. A. Hanson, *Old Kent: The Eastern Shore of Maryland*. Baltimore 1876.

Hesselius, "The family", *Svenskt Biografiskt Lexikon* 18, 1971.

B. Hildebrand, "Nils Collin", *Svenskt Biografiskt Lexikon* 8, 1929.

R. Hulan, "Historiska minnen i Delaware", in Lindberg 1986.

N. Jacobsson, "Johannes Jonae Holmiensis Campanius", *Svenskt Biografiskt Lexikon* 7, 1927.

N. Jacobsson, *Svenska öden vid Delaware, 1638–1831*. Stockholm 1938.

Johnson 1911.

A. Johnson, *Swedish Contributions to American National Life, 1638–1921*. New York 1921.

T.G. Jordan, *American Log Buildings: An Old World Heritage*. Chapel Hill, N.C., and London 1985. (Reviewed by R. H. Hulan in *Swedish American Genealogist*, 1985.)

Kalm 1929.

A. Kastrup, *The Swedish Heritage in America*. St. Paul 1975.

G. B. Keen, *The Descendants of Jöran Kyn of New Sweden*. Philadelphia 1913.

Kero 1986.

O.R. Landelius, *Swedish Place-Names in North America*. Carbondale and Edwardsville, Illinois, 1985.

H. Nelson, *The Swedes and the Swedish Settlements in North America*, Vols. 1–2. Skrifter utg. av Kungl. Humanistiska Vetenskapssamfundet i Lund, 37. Lund 1943.

V. Niitemaa (ed.), *Old Friends – Strong Ties*. Vaasa 1976.

REFERENCES

H.D. Paxson, *Where Pennsylvania History Began.* Philadelphia 1926.

J.E. Pomfret, *The Province of West New Jersey, 1609–1702.* Princeton, N. J., and London 1956.

G.E. Russell, "Anicake/Hanson/Elena/MacKenny Dabb of Kent County, Maryland, 1652–74", *The American Genealogist,* 1978.

"The Swedish settlement in Maryland, 1654", *The American Genealogist,* 1978.

F.D. Scott, *Wertmüller: Artist and Immigrant Farmer.* Chicago 1963.

A. Widen, *Amandus Johnson, svenskamerikan.* Stockholm 1970.

THE FIRST SWEDES IN NEW YORK CITY

V. Berger, "President Roosevelt's Swedish ancestry", *The American Swedish Monthly,* April 1934.

J.O. Evjen, *Scandinavian Immigrants in New York, 1630–1674.* Minneapolis 1916.

Kastrup 1975.

G.V.C. Young, *The Founder of the Bronx.* Peel, Isle of Man, 1981.

SWEDES IN THE AMERICAN WAR OF INDEPENDENCE

H.A. Barton, "Sweden and the War of American Independence", *William and Mary Quarterly,* 1966.

H.A. Barton, *Count Hans Axel von Fersen.* New York 1975.

A.B. Benson, *Sweden and the American Revolution.* New Haven 1926.

S.J. Boëthius, "Oskar II", *Sveriges historia till våra dagar* 13. Stockholm 1925.

K.E. Carlson, *Relations of the United States with Sweden.* Allentown 1921.

H. Elovson, *De svenska officerarna i nordamerikanska frihetskriget.* Scandia 1929.

H. Elovson, *Amerika i svensk litteratur, 1750–1820.* Lund 1930.

I. Hildebrand, *Den svenska kolonin S:t Barthelemy och Västindiska kompaniet fram till 1796.* Lund 1951.

A. Johnson, *Swedish Contributions to American Freedom, 1776–1783,* Vols. 1–2. Philadelphia 1953–57.

THE MASS EMIGRATION 1845 – 1930
THE SWEDISH BACKGROUND

U. Beijbom, *Amerika, Amerika! En bok om utvandringen.* Stockholm 1977.

U. Beijbom, *Guldfeber. En bok om guldrusherna till Kalifornien och Klondike.* Stockholm 1979.

B. Brattne, "Bröderna Larsson: En studie i svensk emigrantagentverksamhet under 1880-talet", *Studia Historica Upsaliensia* 50. Uppsala 1973.

S. Carlsson, "Frikyrklighet och emigration", in *Kyrka, folk, stat: Festskrift till Sven Kjöllerström.* Lund 1967.

S. Carlsson, "Chronology and composition of Swedish emigration to America", in Runblom & Norman 1976.

R. Davidsson, "Den tidiga emigrationen från Kisa socken, 1845–1860", *Svensk 1800-talsemigration. Medd. från Historiska Institutionen i Göteborg* 1. Uppsala 1969.

E. De Geer, "Migration och influensfält: studier av emigration och intern migration i Finland och Sverige, 1816 – 1972", *Studia Historica Upsaliensia* 97. Uppsala 1977.

Emigrationsutredningen. Betänkande och bilagor 1–20. Stockholm 1908–13.

A. Friman, "Svensk utvandring till Nordamerika 1820–1850", *Personhistorisk Tidskrift* 1967.

O. Hellstrom, "Erik Jansson", *Svenskt Biografiskt Lexikon* 20, 1973.

M. Höjfors Hong, "Ölänningar över haven", *Studia Historica Upsaliensia* 143. Uppsala and Stockholm 1986.

O. Isaksson & S. Hallgren, *Bishop Hill. A Utopia on the Prairie.* Stockholm 1969.

H. Johansson, *Folkrörelserna i Sverige.* Stockholm 1980.

A.S. Kälvemark (Ohlander), "Reaktionen mot utvandringen. Emigrationsfrågan i svensk debatt och politik, 1901–1914", *Studia Historica Upsaliensia* 41. Uppsala 1972.

A.S. Kälvemark (Ohlander), (ed.), *Utvandring. Den svenska emigrationen till Amerika i historiskt perspektiv.* Stockholm 1973.

G. Lext, *Studier rörande svensk emigration till Nordamerika, 1850–1880.* Göteborg 1977.

L. Ljungmark, "For sale – Minnesota. Organized promotion of Scandinavian immigration, 1866–1873", *Studia Historica Gothoburgensia* 13. Stockholm 1971.

F. Nilsson, "Emigrationen från Stockholm till Nordamerika, 1880–1893". Monografier utg. av Stockholms Kommunalförvaltning, 31 (= *Studia Historica Upsaliensia* 31). Stockholm 1970.

H. Norman, "Från Bergslagen till Nordamerika", *Studia Historica Upsaliensia* 62. Uppsala 1974.

N.W. Olsson, *Swedish Passenger Arrivals in New York, 1820 – 1850.* Stockholm 1967.

N.W. Olsson, *Swedish Passenger Arrivals in U.S. Ports, 1820 – 1850 (except New York).* St. Paul 1979.

B. Rondahl, "Emigration, folkomflyttning och säsongarbete i ett sågverksdistrikt i södra Hälsingland, 1865–1910", *Studia Historica Upsaliensia* 40. Uppsala 1972.

N. Runeby, "Den nya världen och den gamla: Amerikabild och emigrationsuppfattning i Sverige, 1820–1860", *Studia Historica Upsaliensia* 30. Uppsala 1969.

E. Severin, *Svenskarna i Texas i ord och bild, 1838–1918.* 1919.

REFERENCES

G.M. Stephenson, *The Religious Aspects of Swedish Immigration*. Minneapolis 1932.

K. Söderberg, "Den första massutvandringen: en studie av befolkningsrörlighet och emigration utgående från Alfta socken i Hälsingland, 1846–1895", *Acta Universitatis Umensis* 39. Umeå 1981.

L.G. Tedebrand, "Västernorrland och Nordamerika, 1875–1913. Utvandring och återinvandring", *Studia Historica Upsaliensia* 42. Uppsala 1972.

G. Westin, *Emigranterna och kyrkan*. Stockholm 1932.

A. Wirén, "Uppbrott från örtagård. Utvandring från Blekinge under begynnelsestadiet till och med år 1870", *Bibliotheca Historica Lundensis* 34. Lund 1975.

S. Åkerman, "Theory and methods of emigration research", in Runblom & Norman 1976.

THE SWEDES IN NORTH AMERICA
Fundamental Characteristics

H. Berggren, *Förenta staternas historia*. Stockholm 1966.

N. Hasselmo, *Amerika-Svenska*. Lund 1974.

F. Hedblom, *Svensk-Amerika berättar*. Stockholm 1982.

E. Johansson, "Kvantitativa studier av alfabetiseringen i Sverige", *Historielärarnas Förenings Årsskrift* 1969–70.

S. Lindmark, "Swedish America, 1914–1932. Studies in ethnicity with emphasis on Illinois and Minnesota", *Studia Historica Upsaliensia* 37. Stockholm and Uppsala 1971.

Nelson 1943.

Niitemaa 1976.

R.K. Vedder & L.E. Gallaway, "The settlement preferences of Scandinavian emigrants to the United States, 1850–1960", *The Scandinavian History Economic Review* 1970.

THE SWEDISH SETTLEMENTS IN NORTH AMERICA
Regional Distribution

Beijbom 1979.

P. Fjellström, "Swedish-American colonization in the San Joaquin Valley in California", *Studia Etnographica Upsaliensia* 33. Uppsala 1970.

L. Ljungmark, *Den stora utvandringen. Svensk emigration till USA, 1840–1925*. Stockholm 1965. (English ed.: *Swedish Exodus*, Carbondale, Ill., 1979.)

Nelson 1943.

H. Norman, "Swedes in North America", in Runblom & Norman 1976.

H. Runblom, "Svenskarna i Canada", in *Historieforskning på nya vägar* (ed. L.G. Tedebrand). Lund 1977.

Tedebrand 1972.
Twentieth Census of the United States: Population. 1980.

LOCAL LINKS BETWEEN SWEDEN AND NORTH AMERICA

U. Beijbom, "Swedes in Chicago: a demographic and social study of the 1846–1880 immigration", *Studia Historica Upsaliensia* 38. Växjö and Stockholm 1971.

S. Carlsson (ed.), *Anderstorp*. Uppsala 1980.

U. Ebbeson, *Emigrationen från en bruksbygd i Östergötland*. Unpublished.

N. Hasselmo (ed.), *Perspectives on Swedish Immigration*. Duluth 1978.

Hedblom 1982.

Höjfors Hong 1986.

Kastrup 1975.

B. Lager, "Jacob Fahlström", *Svenskt Biografiskt Lexikon* 15, 1953.

Landelius 1976.

E. Lindquist, *Smoky Valley People: A History of Lindsborg, Kansas*, Augustana Historical Society Publication 13. Lindsborg 1953.

E. Lindquist, *Vision for a Valley: Olof Olsson and the Early History of Lindsborg*, Augustana Historical Society Publication 22. Rock Island 1970.

L. Ljungmark, "Hans Mattson", *Svenskt Biografiskt Lexikon* 25, 1985.

A. Myhrman, *Finlandssvenskar i Amerika*. Skrifter utg. av Svenska Litteratursällskapet i Finland, 453. Helsingfors 1972.

C.E. Måwe, *Värmlänningar i Nordamerika*. Säffle 1971.

Nelson 1943.

Norman 1974.

R.C. Ostergren, "The transplanted Swedish rural immigrant community in the Upper Middle West", in Runblom & Blanck 1986.

J. Redin, J. Johansson et al., *En Smålandssocken emigrerar. En bok om emigrationen till Amerika från Långasjö socken i Kronobergs län*. Växjö 1967.

J.G. Rice, "Marriage behavior and the persistence of Swedish communities in rural Minnesota", in Hasselmo 1978.

H. Runblom 1977.

H. Runblom & D. Blanck (eds.), "Scandinavia Overseas". *Uppsala Multiethnic Papers* 7, 1986.

Tedebrand 1972.

E. Wretlind, *A Swedish Directory of Boston, 1881*. Translated and edited with notes by N. W. Olsson. Winter Park, Fla., 1985. (Reviewed by S. Carlsson in *Personhistorisk Tidskrift* 1987.)

Åkerman 1976.

FARMERS

U. Beijbom, *Utvandrarna och Svensk-Amerika*. Stockholm 1986.

REFERENCES

M. Fries, "Landet som smålänningarna mötte i Amerika", *Natio Smolandica* 1966.

E. Hamberg, "En jämförande undersökning av jordbruk", *Statistisk Tidskrift* 1969.

Kastrup 1975.

Landelius 1985.

Nelson 1943.

Norman 1974.

L. Palmqvist, "Vernacular architecture in Minnesota: Swedish-American farmsteads", in Runblom & Blanck 1986.

ENGINEERS

I. Andersson, *Uddeholms historia*. Stockholm 1960.

A. B. Benson & N. Hedin, *Americans from Sweden*. Philadelphia and New York 1950.

G. Bodman, *Chalmers tekniska institut. Matrikel 1829–1929*. Göteborg 1929.

B. Boëthius & A. Lindström, "Ernst Danielson", *Svenskt Biografiskt Lexikon* 10, 1931.

B. Hildebrand & T. Althin, "John Ericsson", *Svenskt Biografiskt Lexikon* 14, 1951.

G. Indebetou & E. Hylander, *Svenska Teknologföreningen 1881 – 1936*, Vols. 1–2. Stockholm 1937.

Kastrup 1975.

R. Kjellander, "Victor Hybinette", *Svenskt Biografiskt Lexikon* 19, 1972.

B. Lager,"Johan (John) Ernst Ericson", *Svenskt Biografiskt Lexikon* 14, 1951.

J. Liljencrants, "Inventors", in Benson & Hedin 1938.

G. Manasse, "Ivar Svedberg", *Svenska Män och Kvinnor* 7, 1954.

T. Månsson, "John William Nyström", *Svenska Män och Kvinnor* 5, 1949.

S.E. Ohlon, "Hugo Hammar", "Ernst Hedén", *Svenskt Biografiskt Lexikon* 18, 1969–70.

S. Rönnow & G. Törnbom, "Sigfrid Edström", *Svenska Män och Kvinnor* 2, 1944.

S. Sköldberg, "Till blixtlåsets historia", *Daedalus* 1940.

H. E. Westerberg, "Ernst Alexanderson", *Svenskt Biografiskt Lexikon* 1, 1918.

TRANSPORT ACTIVITIES

T. Althin, "Carl Edvard Johansson", *Svenskt Biografiskt Lexikon* 20, 1973.

Articles in Benson & Hedin 1938: by N.G. Sahlin (Soldiers and Sailors), V. E. Freeburg (Imports and Importers), A. A. Stomberg (Pioneers of the Northwest), B. Peterson (Manufacturers), and J. Goldstrom (Aviation).

Benson & Hedin 1950.

G. Blomé, *Twelve Ways to the Top: Swedish-American Success Stories.* New York and Sollentuna 1985.
G. Elgenstierna, *Den introducerade svenska adelns ättartavlor*, 6. Stockholm 1931.
Från månen till värmländsk fädernebygd (Bryggan — The Bridge). Karlstad 1970.
Kastrup 1975.
Norman 1974.
W. Seabrook, *All Europeans.* London 1938.
N. Sundquist, *Martis Jerk, Eric Wickman (1887–1954).* Uppsala 1969.
A. Tjerneld, "Ola Månsson", *Svenskt Biografiskt Lexikon* 26, 1987.

BUILDING CONTRACTORS

Benson & Hedin 1950.
S. Björklund, *Dalfolk i Nordamerika.* Uppsala 1971.
Kastrup 1975.
B. Lager, "Axel Henric (Henry) Ericsson, Nils Johan (John) Emil Ericsson", *Svenskt Biografiskt Lexikon* 14, 1951.
C.T. Larson, "Architects and builders", in Benson & Hedin 1938.
E.G. Westman (ed.), *The Swedish Element in America*, 3. Chicago 1931.

BIG BUSINESSMEN

U. Beijbom 1979.
Blomé 1985.
Kastrup 1975.
T. Månsson, "Carl Johan (Charles John) Alfred Ericson", *Svenskt Biografiskt Lexikon* 14, 1951.

METALWORKERS, CARPENTERS, AND CABINET-MAKERS

Emigrationsutredningen, Bilaga 20. Stockholm 1911.
Beijbom 1971.
Kastrup 1975.
Nelson 1943.

MAIDSERVANTS AND SEAMSTRESSES

Emigrationsutredningen, Bilaga 20. Stockholm 1911.
Beijbom 1971.
W.G. Helmes, *John A. Johnson, the People's Governor.* Minneapolis and London 1949.
Kastrup 1975.
Nelson 1943.

REFERENCES

Nilsson 1970.
A.S. Ohlander, *Kärlek, död och frihet*. Stockholm 1986.

THOSE WHO DISAPPEARED

S. Carlsson, "My American cousins", *Swedish American Genealogist*. 1984.
Redin, Johansson *et al*. 1967.
F. Svedenfors, *Gränsbygden, 2. Mellersta och norra Sunnerbo i gången tid*. Lund
1954.

PASTORS

O.F. Ander, *Tufve Nilsson Hasselquist*, Augustana Library Publications 14.
Rock Island 1931.
G.E. Arden, *Augustana Heritage*. Rock Island 1963.
C. Bergendoff, *Augustana: A Profession of Faith. A History of Augustana College,
1860–1935*, Augustana Library Publication 33. Rock Island 1962.
C. Bergendoff, *The Augustana Ministerium*, Augustana Historical Society Pub-
lication 28, Rock Island 1980. (Reviewed by S. Carlsson in *Historisk
Tidskrift* 1981.)
S. Carlsson, "Augustana Lutheran pastors in the Church of Sweden", *Swed-
ish-American Historical Quarterly* 1984.
Kastrup 1975.
Lindmark 1971.
E. Lindquist, *Shepherd of an Immigrant People: the Story of Erland Carlsson*,
Augustana Historical Society Publication 26. Rock Island 1978.
W. Mulder, *Homeward to Zion: the Mormon Migration from Scandinavia*. Min-
neapolis 1957.
E. Norelius, *De svenska lutherska församlingarnas och svenskarnas historia i
Amerika*, Vols. 1–2. Rock Island 1890–1916. (English edition, Augus-
tana Historical Society Publication 31, Rock Island 1984.)
K.A. Olsson, *By One Spirit: A History of the Evangelical Covenant Church of
America*. Chicago 1962.
S. Rönnegård, *Utvandrarnas kyrka*. Stockholm 1961.
Letters to G.A. Swan, Augustana College, Rock Island, (manuscripts).
W. Wanqvist, "Olof Gustav Hedström", *Svenskt Biografiskt Lexikon* 18, 1970.

THE TWO MAINSTREAMS IN SWEDISH AMERICAN CULTURE
Newspapers and Organizations
Beijbom 1971.
U. Beijbom, "Swedish-American organizational life", in Runblom & Blanck
1986.

F.H. Capps, *From Isolationism to Involvement: the Swedish Immigrant Press in America, 1914–1945*. Chicago 1966.

J. Lincoln, "Charities and self-help", in Benson & Hedin 1938.

Lindmark 1971.

G. Westin, "Johan Alfred Enander", *Svenskt Biografiskt Lexikon* 13, 1950.

SCIENTISTS

A. Barton, *Clio And Swedish America*, in Hasselmo 1978.

U. Beijbom, "Clio i Svensk-Amerika", *Historieforskning på nya vägar* (ed. L.G. Tedebrand). Lund 1977.

A.B. Benson, "Professors", in Benson & Hedin 1938.

Kastrup 1975.

E. Lindquist, *An Immigrant's Two Worlds: A Biography of Hjalmar Edgren*, Augustana Historical Society Publication 23. Rock Island 1972.

T. Månsson, "Johan August Uddén", *Svenska Män och Kvinnor* 8, 1955.

S. Nilsson, "Nobel genealogy visit in Örebro", *The Bridge* 1986.

WRITERS, PAINTERS, AND COMPOSERS

U. Abel, "Carl Milles", *Svenskt Biografiskt Lexikon* 25, 1986.

R. Arvidsson, *Den unge Per Hallström*. Lund 1969.

U. Beijbom, "Vilhelm Berger, en skildrare av emigranternas hundår", *Personhistorisk Tidskrift* 1981.

U. Beijbom 1986.

Benson & Hedin 1950.

S. Ek, "Fredrika Bremer", *Svenskt Biografiskt Lexikon* 6, 1925.

A. Hemming-Sjöberg, *Rättegången mot C.J.L. Almqvist*. Stockholm 1929.

Kastrup 1975.

S. Lagerstedt, *Drömmaren från Norrlandsgatan. En studie i Henning Bergers liv och författarskap*. Monografier utg. av Stockholms Kommunalförvaltning, 25. Stockholm 1963.

Landelius 1985.

E. Lindquist, *An Immigrant's American Odyssey: A Biography of Ernst Skarstedt*, Augustana Historical Society Publication 24. Rock Island 1974.

R. Roos, *Resa till Amerika 1851–55*. Brev utg. av S. Laurell. Stockholm 1969.

D.B. Skårdal, *The Divided Heart: Scandinavian Immigrant Experience Through Literary Sources*. Oslo 1974.

G. Stockenström, "Sociological Aspects of Swedish-American Literature", in Hasselmo 1978.

R. Strombeck, *Leonard Strömberg*. New York 1979.

A. Swanson, "Där ute: Moberg's predecessors", in Hasselmo 1978.

REFERENCES

ACTRESSES AND ACTORS

Articles in Benson & Hedin 1938: by L. Clairmont (Moving Picture Actors), H. Lundbergh (Stage and Radio Performers).

N.O. Franzén, "Johanna (Jenny) Maria Lind", *Svenskt Biografiskt Lexikon* 23, 1980.

Kastrup 1975.

POLITICIANS

O.F. Ander, "Public officials", in Benson & Hedin 1938.

Beijbom 1971.

H. Bengston, *Skandinaver på vänsterflygeln i USA*. Stockholm 1955.

Blomé 1985.

Capps 1966.

S. Carlsson, *Skandinaviska politiker i Minnesota, 1882–1900*. Uppsala 1970.

S. Carlsson, "Scandinavian Politicians in Minnesota around the Turn of the Century", *Americana Norvegica* 3. Oslo 1971.

S. Carlsson, "Politicians", in Runblom & Norman 1976.

Helmes 1949.

N. Hokansson, *Swedish Immigrants in Lincoln's Time*. New York 1942.

Kastrup 1975.

B.L. Larson, *Lindbergh of Minnesota: A Political Biography*. New York 1973.

B.L. Larson, "Swedish Americans and Farmer-Labor Politics in Minnesota", in Hasselmo 1978.

Ljungmark 1971.

R. Lucas, "Charles August Lindbergh, Sr.: a case study of Congressional insurgency, 1906–12", *Studia Historica Upsaliensia* 61. Uppsala 1974.

G.H. Mayer, *The Political Career of Floyd B. Olson*. Minneapolis 1951.

T. Månsson, "Fredrik (Frederick) Lundin", *Svenska Män och Kvinnor* 5, 1949.

P. Nordahl, *De sålde sina penslar. Om några svenska målare som emigrerade till USA*. Stockholm, 1987.

M.W. Odland, *The Life of Knute Nelson*. Minneapolis 1926.

Rondahl 1972.

G.M. Stephenson, *John Lind of Minnesota*. Minneapolis 1935.

I. Söderström, *Joe Hill, diktare och agitator*. Stockholm 1970.

J. Weibull, "The Wisconsin Progressives, 1900–1916", *Mid-America* 47, 1965.

Who's Who in American Politics, 1985–1986, Tenth Ed. New York 1985.

J.M. Youngdale, "Populism, Democracy and Paradigm Shift", *American Studies in Scandinavia* 1986.

CONCLUSIONS

Kastrup 1975.

INDEX

PERMANENT AND TEMPORARY
SWEDISH AMERICANS

ACKNOWLEDGEMENTS

I thank warmly Peter Wallenberg for the first suggestion of writing a survey of Swedish achievements in North America; New Sweden´88 and Svenska Institutet for making this project financially possible; Peter Hammarström and Ulla Rasch-Anderson for their helpfulness at the first stage of the work; Bo and Anna Streiffert, Christina von Sivers, and Turlough Johnston for a fine cooperation during the final stages.
Uppsala, in December 1987
Sten Carlsson

Cover ill.: Claes Forsslöf; **Endpapers:** Riksarkivet; **Page 14**: Emigrantsinst., Växjö; **17** Kungl. Biblioteket, Sthlm.; **20, 25**: The American Swedish Hist. Museum, Philadelphia; **33**: Nordiska Museet, Sthlm.; **36**: Östergötlands Länsmuseum; **40 — 41**: Långasjö Emigrantcirkel; **44 — 45**: "The Swedes and the Swedish settlements in North America"; **48**: "En smålandssocken emigrerar"; **57**: Nordiska Museet, Sthlm.; **61**: Pressens Bild; **62**: Sjöfartsmuseet, Göteborg; **65**: Tekniska Museet, Sthlm.; **69, 70**: Pressens Bild; **75**: "The Swedish Element in America II"; **79**: "The Swedish Element in America IV"; **80, 81**: Emigrantinst., Växjö; **84**: Sjöfartsmuseet, Göteborg; **89**: "The Swedish Element in America I"; **91**: Gullers Pictorial/K.W. Gullers; **94**: "The Swedish Element in America II"; **98**: Emigrantregistret, Karlstad; **103, 104, 106**: Pressens Bild; **113**: Minnesota Hist. Society; **117**: Svenskt Pressfoto; **119**: Pressens Bild.

NOVA SUECIA : Eller the Swenska RE[...]

Sickpeckxas Sippus

Reeb und bredh Sö, eller
Häwiskakimensj.
Röcklebonsbörn.
Lillefalcökylen.

Ackan Ramangehä
Saseckhocknug

Koyaka Salunge

Uslargen kylen.
Opinur Rz Vddra.

Anckr Rykylen.
Mingues Kyd: eller Apoque tnema

Bomtienb Uddru.
Häger Vddra.

24.

25. eller Kilbernadh Kylen.

Drusset Vddru.

Elsbe
Oytses Singsi
Korten Reviter 27.

26.

Mesnisano
Narrayticons Kyl. Wiwe

Lamtelkylen.
Kagaikarizachien.

Tammenb Eylands.
Sepattackingh   Alamohackingh.

Asbveticans Revier
eller Riddarr Kylen.

Scala Mil: Germ: 15 in uno Gradu.

1   2   3   4   5

nn kallab Treefaldig[...]forts Fort. C: Niew Elavelands. D: Neandwijck. E: Teanr Vdden. F: Lil falcöden G: Christinakyl. H: Sisteir kylen...
...ern Vddra, Senlockan. Rasmensj menanchitonna. og marineckyl. J: Sfinlands. 11: Wplands. W. Stillens vh. X: Teanakonck. 11: [...]kl: eller
De Beoninghackingh. 7. Sechansio Eylands. 8. Mechopinackan. 9. Rophakelky. 10. Asbajungh. 11. Tinterenckb Eylands. 12: Marachon sien
angsvddn. 25. Ragaikaraekiens Sippus. 26. Obissqualoit. 27. Asamohackingökyl.